LEAD

Building Connection, Community, and Collaboration for WOMEN IN BUSINESS

AliceAnne Loftus

Featuring Leading Lady Ambassadors

Blamphin, Jennifer Bonk, Michelle Briggs, Julie Campbell,
ille Campins-Adams, Erin Harrigan, Elizabeth Harris,
ennifer Osterhouse, Maureen Porto, Emily Reagan,
hrissy Rey, Michelle Ternstra, Lisa M. Van Wormer

"An extremely encouraging collection of powerful narratives from 14 remarkable and real women in business. From the very first page, I was captivated by the raw authenticity of these women. No pretends and no filters. Their unique stories are not just about professional achievements but also about a diversity of personal and emotional experiences that shaped their professional journey. Reading about their struggles and accomplishments made me feel deeply connected, understood, and not alone.

These women converge on a common thread of resilience, perseverance, and determination. This book is a piece of evidence on the power of community and connection.

You'll find yourself cheering for these women, empathizing with their experiences, and celebrating their victories. Moreover, the book offers valuable lessons and practical tips for you to succeed, making it not just a source of inspiration but also a practical guide for any woman considering a business or already working in growing their business.

It's a celebration of female entrepreneurship, and a reminder that when we see each other as allies, collaborators, and partners, amazing and magical things happen.

This book left me feeling validated and inspired to lead my own unique journey."

~ Maria Winters, LCPC, NCC and Founder of The Coaching Therapist

*

"In *We Lead*, the collective wisdom of these inspiring women shines. Their stories remind us that in unity and authenticity, we find the keys to success. This book beautifully illustrates the power of women supporting women and the incredible outcomes that result from collaboration."

~ Katrina Campins, The Campins Company, Luxury Real Estate Specialist, Fox Business/Fox News Real Estate Contributor, Host of Mansion Global on Fox Business PRIMETIME!

*

"The voices within *We Lead* resonate with the power of collaboration and authenticity. These remarkable women demonstrate that true leadership is grounded in community and a commitment to making a difference. This expert collaboration offers valuable insights into the world of authentic leadership and the strength of women coming together."

~ Elizabeth Hambleton, Bestselling Author, Speaker, and CEO of Bonjour Branding

*

"*We Lead* is a must-read for any woman in business. This book is fun and engaging. It shows common leadership challenges from a variety of different industries. I found myself pleasantly surprised at how it was more stories than lectures, but loved "The Practice" sections at the end of each chapter. It felt like I was a part of the family but had specific action items to complete for my business, if I wanted to. I also love that I was given ways to contact the co-authors if I wanted to learn more. Do your business a favor and go read this book.

~ Tara De Leon, MS, RSCC, CSCS*D, USAW, NASM-PES, FMSC, GGS CPPC, Personal Training Coordinator

Building Connection, Community, and Collaboration *for* WOMEN IN BUSINESS

AliceAnne Loftus

Featuring Leading Lady Ambassadors

Julie Blamphin, Jennifer Bonk, Michelle Briggs, Julie Campbell,
Camille Campins-Adams, Erin Harrigan, Elizabeth Harris,
Jennifer Osterhouse, Maureen Porto, Emily Reagan,
Chrissy Rey, Michelle Terpstra, Lisa M. Van Wormer

We Lead
Building Connection, Community, and Collaboration for Women in Business
AliceAnne Loftus
©Copyright 2023 AliceAnne Loftus
Published by Brave Healer Productions
Paperback ISBN: 978-1-961493-11-7
eBook ISBN: 978-1-961493-06-3

DISCLAIMER

This book offers words of wisdom with regard to physical, mental, emotional, and spiritual wellbeing and is designed for educational purposes only. You should not rely on this information as a substitute for, nor does it replace professional medical or business advice, diagnosis, or treatment. If you have concerns or questions about your health, business, or mental wellbeing, you should always consult with a physician, other healthcare professional, or business professional. Do not disregard, avoid or delay obtaining medical or business-related advice from your healthcare or business professional because of something you may have read here. The use of any information provided in this book is solely at your own risk.

Developments in research may impact the health, business, and life advice that appears here. No assurances can be given that the information contained in this book will always include the most relevant findings or developments with respect to the particular material.

Having said all that, know that the authors here have shared their tools, practices, and knowledge with you with a sincere and generous intent to assist you on your journey to being unstoppable in business and life. Please contact them with any questions you may have about the techniques or information they have provided. They will be happy to assist you further!

DEDICATION

*To every member of the Leading Lady community,
you deserve to take up space. Thanks for showing up
for yourself and each other.*

TABLE OF CONTENTS

INTRODUCTION | i

INTRODUCTION

I'm absolutely thrilled to share the remarkable journey of the Leading Lady Ambassador program, which had its humble beginnings in 2019.

"I need to connect with more like-minded women business owners." A fellow business owner shared with me one day over lunch. "I just feel like we could learn so much from each other, and I'm tired of feeling so alone in all this."

"I have an idea!" I beamed. The idea was simple yet powerful. I immediately got to work creating a "business mastermind" comprised of a group of exceptional women whom I frequently recommended for their expertise.

The ambassadors weren't just a random selection; they were women in business with whom I shared personal experiences. From website developers to marketing experts and those who provided invaluable guidance in navigating parenthood, I knew these women to be exceptional in their fields and deeply committed to their customers' welfare. With this profound trust and faith in their capabilities, I confidently referred them to others, knowing they'd deliver nothing short of excellence. As we convened for our monthly meetings, the energy in the room was palpable, and together, we brainstormed innovative ways to support our community. We fostered a vibrant referral circle, exchanging business opportunities and connecting each other with our extensive networks and clientele. It was an unequivocal win for everyone involved.

Our mission was twofold: to strategize and plan for the upcoming year and then extend our support and resources to the larger Leading Lady community. These incredible women, who played pivotal roles in both my personal and professional life, formed the heart and soul of the ambassador program, becoming an integral part of the Leading Lady brand. Together, we forged an unbreakable bond, tirelessly empowering and uplifting each other's businesses and establishing a dynamic network that proved beneficial to us all.

As the program blossomed, we witnessed incredible growth and success, but nothing could've prepared us for the challenges that lay ahead in 2020. The world came to a screeching halt, and we had to adapt quickly to navigate the new digital landscape. Businesses all over the world adjusted, pivoted, and searched for innovative ways to continue operating. Amidst the uncertainty, the ambassadors stepped up to support one another, creating a safe space for business owners to share their struggles and triumphs. It was during this transformative period that we discovered the true power of connection and collaboration. We shared ideas on how to launch online programs, move in-person events to virtual summits and workshops, and empower ourselves with financial awareness and strategic planning to overcome the challenges that came with the uncharted terrain of operating businesses during a global pandemic.

The strength, support, encouragement, and perspective shared between us all changed our businesses in ways we couldn't even imagine. In a time that could've easily broken us all, we learned we could take our businesses to new horizons: offer programs and services we hadn't thought of in the traditional ways we did business, reach audiences, clients, and collaborators outside of our geographical locations, and uplift and encourage business owners and women leaders to adjust and adapt with us. Our goal wasn't too merely "survive"; we knew we could thrive.

Now, with the program soaring to new heights and expanding nationally, I'm in awe of the collective energy and dedication of these inspiring women. The Leading Lady Ambassadors are not just a collection of businesses and brands; they're the very heartbeat of our mission—connecting, educating, and inspiring women in business and leadership. I feel blessed to lead this incredible group, and I can't wait to share more about our exciting journey together. As we continue to grow and evolve, I'm confident that the Leading Lady Ambassador program will leave an indelible mark on the lives of countless women, empowering them to thrive, innovate, and lead in their respective fields. Together, we're creating a powerful force of change, building a brighter future for women entrepreneurs everywhere. As you read their stories, you'll learn powerful and impactful practices and strategies that you'll be able to apply immediately to your business, organization, and life. Grab your pen, scribble notes as you read along, and know that you're never alone on your journey.

Chapter 1

LEADING LADIES

Proof that Community Over Competition Wins Every Time

AliceAnne Loftus, Business and Leadership Coach

MY STORY

Let's be honest; I love a good "Boss Babe" party. Hang the banners, cue the confetti, and wear your brightest, sparkliest pink pumps, and let's dance the night away to Beyonce's *Run the World (Girls)*. It's fun and cute to don phrases like "girl gang," "lady boss," and "business besties." There's an exuberant and celebratory energy when you think of women getting together to hype each other up. I *love* the sisterhood of it all. What's not to love? I want to feel like we're in it together, building each other up, making room for one another's successes, and softening the falls and fumbles without judgment or criticism. It's easy to spit out cliches about women supporting women. It's another thing to support women in business, leadership, and life. It takes self-awareness, confidence, compassion, and dedication to be the kind of woman who mentions another woman's name in a room full of opportunities. The ability to release your own ego and commit to the idea that "a rising tide lifts all boats" is something many say, yet few practice.

"I'm not sure I belong here," a woman whispered as she entered one of the Leading Lady's monthly networking and education meetings. Her eyes darted around the room as she shrunk back, trying to appear small and hidden. "The women here have it all together. I'm not confident, prepared, or established. What could I possibly have to offer?"

"Nonsense!" I gasped back at her. "If you think all these women here aren't ready to receive you with open arms, you don't understand what it means to be a Leading Lady." I put my arm around her and felt her body relax just a bit, but as fast as she softened, I felt her stiffen back up. It was as if she just couldn't hold her breath a moment longer and needed to get a little out to suck in another inhalation.

Truthfully, I knew exactly how this woman felt. I've always felt like somewhat of an outsider. I just never quite "fit." I can't even count the number of times I longed to belong. Growing up, I was an odd duck as the only Asian American in my school. I had trouble relating to others, and even within my own family, I wasn't Filipino enough to connect and appreciate the culture of my mother, and I wasn't white enough to understand the privilege inherited from my white father. In my early years, I couldn't quite put my finger on why, but I knew that I was different, and I was hell-bent on trying to figure out how I could get an invitation to a seat at the table with the others.

I spent the next twenty years trying to earn my seat. I compared myself to others, and I tried on different masks to hide who I really was, hoping to blend in with what I thought others wanted me to be. I measured my worth by how I measured up to others. If someone turned away from me, I absorbed the fault and shame. *I'm not good enough. Try harder. Figure out what they want you to be so you can be included.*

I'm willing to bet that more women than not, at one point or another felt insecure, less than, out of place, unwelcomed, and even like they were just an imposter in a room full of shiny people. It's a horrible feeling. It's jarring. It triggers every fight-and-flight response imaginable. For me, I retreat, shrink back, hide, and make excuses as to why I need to leave. There are even times I've done worse; I fake it, I slap on a giant smile to mask my pain, and play the loop of negative self-talk: *I'm not good enough. Try harder. Figure out what they want you to be so you can be included.* It's an incredible pain. I'd go as far as to say it probably stopped many women dead in their tracks from stepping out of their comfort zones and living and leading to their full potential. No one wants to feel vulnerable, and no one wants to be rejected. It's precisely because I'm all too familiar with these feelings that I make it my life's work to be sure that every woman I encounter knows she matters. I have a visceral reaction to the feelings of not belonging, being sized up, and then either deemed a threat or even inconsequential. I've been on the receiving end too often in my life not to be acutely aware that I can impact whether a woman feels included or invisible.

Much of the narrative around being a "Girl Boss" is that we're tired of being mansplained, pushed aside with a pat on the head, belittled, disregarded, and minimized because we're women. I admit, there's no doubt that sexism and gender discrimination are real and very much do happen. However, I've had more experiences of being shut down, turned away, discounted, or made to feel small by more women than men.

The mean junior high girls sneered, "Did you see her knock off Keds? She buys them at K-Mart. What a loser." I was left ashamed, embarrassed, and feeling completely inferior as I tucked my white canvas-covered feet under my chair, hiding the evidence that my family was somehow poor. I pleaded with my parents to buy me the real name brands. "Mom, everyone is making fun of me!" I'd cry. "When you have a job and bills of your own, you can decide to spend your money on frivolous fashion," she would answer.

It was the "popular girls" whispering, giggling, and pointing, "Someone's on the rag." Or "Aunt Flo has come to visit; better plug her up," as I walked down the hall with my sweatshirt tied around my waist because my period bled through my white shorts. "Gross. She probably bled all over the chairs. Someone call the janitor! Clean up in Room B3 Algebra, please!" As if I was the only female to ever have a menstruation mishap. Only losers let the world know their bodies do natural things.

"Your breasts are going to be hideous empty tube socks," The mom at Baby & Me music classes said as I nursed my daughter. "Your children will be insecure because you let a babysitter be with them so much while you work." Another mother disapprovingly inserted. The constant mom-shaming and should-ing all over each other is heavy and tiresome. I began to question everything I did as a young mother.

"She's a gold digger," the lady I met at a neighborhood party rumored that I must have married my husband for money after she learned we had a significant age difference. "There's only one reason a woman her age is interested in a man his age. I hope he has a prenup."

"Supporting women in business isn't a real thing; she's just doing it for attention," a woman gossiped about my businesses and my intentions. "The businesses she supports aren't even real; they are just for women's hobbies or for women who can't secure real careers."

Every encounter, exchange, and interaction helped shape the narrative that no matter what I was doing, I was doing it wrong, and I'd never be doing anything right. Women were out to get each other. If I win, she loses; if I show my weaknesses, she will pounce. Why is that? My guess: we were taught at a very young age that we are competitors. If she's better, faster, prettier, or more intelligent than me, she wins, and I lose. There's no room for both of us.

After most of my life surviving this narrative, I thought: *I have to do better. We have to do better!* I started to change how I interacted with women. I got curious. I started seeing the women around me as my allies, collaborators, and partners. I began to understand that if my win came at the cost of another woman, it was no longer a win. A true victory is when you help other women win; incredible things happen when we win together. I wanted to create something where women ready to truly live this narrative and build each other up could connect and collaborate. I was prepared to drop the drive toward competition and find my community; if I couldn't, I would build it.

Building a community takes commitment and patience. The Leading Lady community started small. I started with my local

MeetUp, a social platform that helps you organize meetings and gatherings in your neighborhood, and invited women to meet me in coffee shops and restaurants. Each week anywhere from two to twelve women would meet up with me for about an hour. Some women knew me from my childcare business that I started in 2004, but as the weeks passed, more women who never heard of me found me through the app. During our meetups, we discussed topics I felt were relevant to women in leadership, and then I offered resources the women could take back to their lives and businesses. I wouldn't call these lectures but rather discussions. Each woman shared her experiences and offered insight on the topics. We discussed such issues as balancing motherhood and building a career, time management, setting boundaries, and conflict resolution. The women began supporting one another through encouragement, validating shared feelings, and helpful resources and connections. I hope they felt a little more grounded, supported, and inspired. I saw the immediate impact this made on each woman, which fueled my drive to keep going.

In 2018, I launched a "Women in Leadership Series" and hosted ten workshops at a venue in my city. Each event had approximately 30-60 women in attendance. I hosted guest speakers on various topics, organized activities and experiences that we could share, and grew the Leading Lady network by the hundreds by the end of the year. I realized I needed a place for all the women I met in person to connect online. Out of sheer convenience and accessibility, I created the Leading Lady Facebook Group. At first, I just used it as a place for the women to connect further after meeting in person. Then, I started posting the topics and continuing the discussions online when some women couldn't attend our meetups and events. Before I knew it, members started adding and inviting their friends, coworkers, relatives, and every other woman they knew from all around the world to the online group. It snowballed into an online community where women could go to inspire or be inspired. It was a powerful thing to watch unfold and bloom. In 2023, our community has nearly 6,500 members, and it's still growing.

What I see as more women show up to support other women is that it cultivates more inclusivity by empowering the individuals and the group. I witness solidarity, leading to stronger social connections and networks. We're challenging the "mean girl" narrative and advocating for the community over competition. I'm dedicated to fostering a culture of collaboration. I invite women to drop the "queen bee" mentality, work cooperatively to link arms and commit to working together to inspire positive change and create a better future for ourselves and future generations. Over the years, I often receive messages, emails, and phone calls from women stating they feel higher confidence, self-esteem, and a sense of empowerment. They're so grateful for a supportive environment where they feel valued and capable. They think they've finally found a place where they truly belong. As women connect online, it often involves mentoring and guiding each other, especially in professional settings. There are numerous situations where this mentorship was invaluable in helping women advance in their careers, pursue leadership roles, and even start their own businesses. Witnessing this impact is inspiring and evidence that through cooperation, connection, and collaboration, women are forging forward and stepping into more leadership roles with confidence and assurance.

Problems solved, right? *Not quite.*

We cannot deny that women face unique challenges and barriers due to gender discrimination. While there's much to say, I'll leave that to another discussion. I was conscientious that the platform could quickly shift to a place where women complained, vented, commiserated, and aired grievances. That's a natural progression in conversation when you get together with a group of individuals with similar challenges. We all want to feel validated, seen, and less alone in our plight. We've also seen carnage when women contribute to the barriers by competing, attacking, and minimizing each other. Because I carefully curated relevant topics, asked empowering questions, and invited discussions focused on problem-solving, the group's energy gravitated towards a more uplifting and optimistic perspective of encouragement and empowerment rather than a victim mentality. It attracted more positive energy, and I began to see the impact in the community and beyond. Supporting one another can help overcome these obstacles by providing resources, sharing experiences, and advocating for change. We can ally ourselves and challenge those stereotypes and gender biases. We can work together to advocate for gender equality, women's rights, and issues that disproportionately affect women.

It doesn't stop there; it can lead to increased economic empowerment when women support women in business and entrepreneurship. Encouraging women-owned businesses and promoting their products and services can contribute to economic growth and gender equality. This can create a positive ripple effect in families and communities. Empowered women are more likely to support their families and contribute to the well-being of their communities. Nothing better illustrates this than a text message I received from a friend after a local magazine announced their "Best of" businesses:

"Have you seen the 'Best of' List? There are so many Leading Lady businesses on it! Great job encouraging us all to support women-owned businesses. It's working!"

I admit I was overwhelmed with a sense of pride. Pride that the values that brought the community together also propelled the recognition and appreciation of many women-owned businesses in our area. Businesses are shared, celebrated, referred to, and mentioned throughout the network, making our community tighter, closer, and more intimate despite the ever-growing numbers of members and participation. I've seen the collaboration firsthand because I do business with many women I've met through the Leading Lady community. This is actually how the Leading Lady Ambassador program was formed.

The Ambassadors are women entrepreneurs with whom I have personally worked and are committed to the highest standards to best support other women. When people ask me who I work with in various aspects of my life and business, I have a group of vetted professionals I'd recommend a million times without hesitation. Need a web developer? *Let me put you in touch with Chrissy Rey; she's built three incredible websites for me.* Want to know how I get such beautiful graphic designs for my program? *Sure! I'll connect you with Jennifer Osterhouse.* Want to know how I finally ditched diet culture? *Let me introduce you to Elizabeth Harris.* The simplicity of it is that many of my ideal clients and customers are also the perfect clients and customers of many of the Ambassadors. However, I'm only an expert in my niche as a business and leadership coach. My clients' vast needs far exceed my skills, knowledge, and experience. To best serve my clients, I feel that it's my responsibility to share resources, connections, and the services of others that can best support those vast needs. Sharing those referrals and resources is collaborating with my network to serve the greater needs of all. This is the perfect example of how when we work together, everyone wins: My client wins because she's getting connected to the resources and support she needs in many areas of her life, and the members of the network win because they're connecting with clients they're excited to work with. I win because the women around me are winning and appreciate that I introduced them! If I tried to work in a bubble, worried that other women were my competitors, or acted out of fear or insecurity, none of us would prosper.

The actual definition of "networking" is the action or process of interacting with others to exchange information and develop professional or social contacts. Networking isn't just about referrals of business, though. Sure, we can share business by building an extensive network, but it's so much more than that. It's the shared knowledge and experiences as well. I think that's what's missing from many network organizations and groups. We may have found ourselves at one time or another attending a networking luncheon. You know, the luncheon hosted in a private room at a restaurant or hotel conference room, and you spend about ninety minutes to two hours listening to a presenter share about their business, hearing others' 30-second elevator pitches, and walking out with a stack of new business cards that'll either be lost in the bottom of our work bag or filed away in a drawer only to be wrapped in a rubber band with a stack of 100 others and never looked at again? Sounds kind of grim, doesn't it? Honestly, I guess it *can* be effective. Obviously, it's working for a lot of people. It's not what fills my cup or what I envisioned for the Leading Lady community. I wanted more collaboration, connection, shared experiences, and support. I wanted to hear stories of how businesses were started, how these women plan to scale or expand, and how they overcame challenges and celebrated successes. Why? Because through shared stories, we learn from one another. We gain insight into how others have moved before us, we're inspired to take action on our own path, and we pave the way for others to follow when they're scared to take their next step. We're not meant to do this alone. While we're each on our own journey, knowing we have the support and encouragement of our networks is where it becomes our community. It's no longer a race, competition, or winner takes all; it's a collaboration to lift each other up, expand possibilities, open opportunities, and be greater together.

If you know me, you know I love a good party. You know the music plays, a banner hangs, and confetti is strewn about. There are a lot of pink signs that read "empowered women, empower women," and there are a lot of hugs. My heels are kicked off, and I'm running to meet you at the door to welcome you with open arms. I've often compared the Leading Lady community to entering a room with a long banquet table where everyone brings their unique dish to share. We're not comparing casseroles or participating in a competition of marmalades; no, it's not that at all. We're creating a feast to feed many. We all have our strengths, talents, and skills ("prized dishes," so to speak). The table is bountiful. There's plenty for all. However, it's not just what's *on* the table that matters; it's who's *around* it. The table is never ending, continually expanding, and forever creating and holding space for whoever wants to pull up a chair. There's room for you here. No competition, just community

THE PRACTICE

Let's talk about how to actually create a community. It's more than just sending out an invitation and hoping people show up and magically sync with the vibe. There are a few crucial points to consider. Whether you're hosting in-person meetings and events or creating a group or network on a social media platform, there are ten fundamental principles I've implemented as well as observed in the Leading Lady community:

1. Creating Safe Spaces: Establishing safe and supportive spaces where women can openly discuss challenges and seek guidance without fear of judgment.

2. Networking and Collaboration: Encourage networking among women in various fields and industries. Building strong connections can lead to collaborative opportunities and partnerships that benefit everyone involved.

3. Addressing Stereotypes: Women can work together to challenge and dismantle harmful stereotypes and biases that might affect their advancement. Educating and supporting each other can create a more inclusive environment. Don't be silent when stereotypes are shared. Speak up and stand up against it.

4. Advocacy for Equal Opportunities: Women can advocate for equal opportunities and representation in various spheres of life, including leadership positions, industries, and policymaking.

5. Support for Entrepreneurship: Encouraging and supporting female entrepreneurship is another essential

aspect of practicing community over competition. By promoting women-led businesses and startups, the community can thrive collectively.

6. Mentorship and Support: Women can actively engage in mentorship programs to support other women in their personal and professional growth. By sharing knowledge, experiences, and guidance, they can help uplift each other and break down barriers that might hinder their progress.

7. Collaborative Projects: Collaborating on projects, initiatives, or community service activities can strengthen bonds among women and lead to meaningful impacts.

8. Sharing Resources: Whether it's sharing career opportunities, access to networks, or knowledge, women can actively contribute to each other's success by sharing resources that can elevate their collective standing.

9. Celebrate Achievements: Women should celebrate each other's achievements without hinting at envy or rivalry. Acknowledging and celebrating success creates a positive and empowering atmosphere within the community.

10. Empowering Future Generations: Women can work together to empower and inspire the next generation of girls and young women to pursue their dreams fearlessly, creating a legacy of community support.

By embracing these principles, women can create more robust networks and contribute to a more inclusive and supportive environment. The power of community lies in the collective efforts to uplift one another, and when *we* come together, *WE LEAD* the way toward positive change and empowerment.

With an entrepreneurial spirit ingrained from an early age, AliceAnne has been a successful business owner for nearly two decades. As she navigated her own path in business and leadership, she discovered a deep calling to uplift and support other women in their pursuits of success. Through her journey, she realized the profound impact connections and community with other women can have on personal and professional growth. Guided by the belief that empowered women empower women, she embarked on a mission to create spaces that fostered collaboration and support among women.

AliceAnne's dedication to building connections, supporting women, and advocating for empowerment has positioned her as a community leader. Her journey has shown that through the power of community, women can find inspiration, strength, and the courage to lead with authenticity.

In her personal and professional endeavors, AliceAnne Loftus continues to exemplify the belief that building strong connections, collaborations, and community with women is the key to unlocking their limitless potential.

Join AliceAnne and the Leading Lady community at https://www.facebook.com/groups/LeadingLadiesAAL

Chapter 2

MY BODY IS MY BUSINESS

The Art and Science of Yoga to Cultivate Self-Connection, Stability, and Success

Julie Blamphin, Inspirational Speaker,
Founder of Stretch Your Spirit

MY STORY

Self-Care is So Cliché

It was a Thursday in May 2013 when I lost my hearing. That day at 4 pm, I felt my ear pop. If you've ever been in an airplane, you know what I mean. This didn't alarm me; I just opened my mouth really wide and wiggled my jaw. Then I'll never forget what happened next. Two hours later, I was sitting on my meditation cushion in my groovy little home yoga studio—the lights were low, and the candles were lit—guiding a private client through restorative poses when I noticed the music volume on my little

Logitech speaker was turning down without me touching it. That seemed strange, but I thought the battery was dying, so I simply turned the volume (back) up. At about 8 pm, I noticed the ringing in my right ear. Now I was paying attention. *What the fuck? I can't get sick right now. I'm leaving tomorrow for my annual week with Momma in Florida!*

Little did I know about what was yet to come. Another two hours later, vertigo hit me so hard I couldn't see straight or stand up without falling. *Am I having a stroke, or am I losing my mind?* It felt like pure chaos.

"Get on my back."

"No, babe. I can't stand up."

I had crumpled to the floor on my hands and knees, wondering why my eyes kept darting side-to-side. I was terrified.

"Get on my back, Jules, now."

My boyfriend Stash reached around me with both arms.

You can do this. Your body is your business. You are balanced. You are stable.

My inner voice (typically bitchy, when speaking to myself) was pointing me toward the positive.

Plant one foot. He's got you. Move from a place of power. Exhale, energize, and rise.

Accepting his loving help and trusting my inner voice, I was able to get to my feet. Leaning on him like a backpack, Stash walked me gently down the flight of stairs, sat me on the bottom stoop, and ran through the summer night to fetch the car.

I dropped my head in my hands and cried.

The Balance Beam Kid

As soon as we headed for the hospital, I dialed my mother and held the phone to my right ear, but it seemed to immediately drop the call. I redialed, held it to my right ear again, then switched it to my left.

"...aren't you answering me? Honey? Jupee? Are you there?"

I burst into fresh tears. The moment I heard Momma was in mid-sentence is when I realized I didn't have hearing on my right side.

When you lose your hearing, there's nothing they can do for you at the hospital. After testing proved negative for a stroke, I waited on a gurney in the emergency room from 11 pm until 3 am. They then sent me home with prescriptions for a sedative, an anti-nausea medication, and the recommendation that I cancel my trip. *Nooo, not my week with Momma.* I was informed my inner ear was damaged, but the elevation of a flight might damage it further.

The days that followed were both frustrating and fascinating. Because the inner ear helps to regulate balance, I couldn't walk right for a week and couldn't drive for a month. The fact that my balance now sucked was (and still is) a big deal for me. Balance was my jam! I've been a yoga teacher for fifteen years, plus I grew up in a school of gymnastics and have been practicing balance my entire life. My childhood consisted of school, playtime, chores, and practice.

"The Farm" was nestled in a sprawling green valley on twenty-three acres in Caledonia, New York. When my parents bought the property, there were three horses, six hens, one old dog named Dixie, and a bantam rooster who chased me around when I was a toddler.

Evidently, the gymnastics school plan began when a lady up the road asked my mother to teach her daughter a cartwheel. Momma received her college degree in physical education, and word spreads quickly in a small town. Soon there were twelve girls practicing cartwheels in our living room. Before long, the farm animals were sold, and my parents created and maintained the most successful school of gymnastics in western New York.

I was in the gym every day from the age of six to sixteen. Dad used to call me the Balance Beam Kid. When I was eleven, I placed third on beam in the state of New York. The judges never gave me a perfect 10, but I could hold a handstand longer than most and a headstand longer than everyone. Trust me when I say that balance was my jam. Clearly, it's not anymore.

No Known Cause

How have I handled my hearing loss? Not well, at least, not at first.

I was perplexed and totally depressed. Both an audiologist and an ear, nose, and throat doctor told me what I already knew – that I had a profound and total hearing loss in my right ear. Be that as it may, they couldn't give me the answer to my question: *Why?*

"Have you had a cold lately?"

"No, Doc."

"Car accident?"

"Nope."

"How about scuba diving? Have you been scuba diving recently?"

"No, I haven't been scuba diving recently."

"Hmm." *Looks at notes again.*

Idiopathic: (adjective) arising from an unknown cause (1)

Grrreat. No known cause. Thanks for nothing. What a lame and unpleasant diagnosis.

But when life hands you lemons, you make lemonade, right? Whatever. I prefer a margarita. *I can hear my parents' voices loud and clear: "She's a rebel and a black sheep. She dances to her own drum."*

Since that idiopathic diagnosis felt so amiss, I decided to find closure *my* way. I could persevere and stay pissed, but as my leadership coach AliceAnne Loftus says, "You can only control two things: your attitude and your effort." (2) I chose to explore my challenge from a different perspective.

(In)Stability

Not all challenges are simply physical. How can they be? We are physical, mental, emotional, sexual, spiritual, and energetic human beings. It's all connected. Having that perspective spurred me to ask myself some tough questions.

What should I be hearing? Can I be a better listener? Am I as balanced as I can be?

These questions led to journaling, followed by contemplations and then meditations. My yoga mat and I spent more time together than ever.

Feeling good was my daily goal, but it was impossible with tinnitus (ear ringing) and vertigo. I was constantly distracted and immersed in negative thoughts about my *new way of being.* According to the Mayo Clinic, "Spending too much time… thinking negative or random thoughts can be draining. It can also make you more likely to experience stress, anxiety, and symptoms of depression." (3)

I enrolled immediately in a course that's deeply rooted in the tradition and practice of yoga. On my last day of training in Mindfulness-Based Stress Reduction, I was sitting on a cushion in a calm, quiet space at the Insight Meditation Center in Washington DC, and thought: *I'm so happy to be right here in this moment. I'm starting to feel good again!* But as it turned out, my head started reeling just a few minutes later. *Stay in the moment. Breathe. Connect with self. Ugh! This is hard. One step forward and three steps back. Is this really my journey for the rest of my life?*

To be honest, I used to think the term *self-care* was so cliché. I've always lived on the wild side—reckless and free! Yes, I'm relatively healthy, but salty snacks are my favorite food group, I don't drink in moderation, I'm a light sleeper, I use the cheapest hair products, I cuss a *lot*, and I drive way too fast. *Note to Self: Just because you can, doesn't mean you should.*

I figured that all stems from a place of fear. I've never wanted to be gentle with myself, but that's what I teach my yogis, so perhaps I should start practicing what I preach. Despite everything, my body is my business, so it was time to slow the fuck down and get real. It was time to make some changes. Even though the diagnosis was idiopathic, one doesn't just lose one's hearing for no reason. I started listening better to others and also to my own body. I started practicing balance with a vengeance. And by *balance*, I don't mean just standing on one foot. Every single day, in real life, I practiced balance: carrying my bags on one shoulder and then the other, scheduling my time between work and play, and even switching the cross of my legs while sitting. I was in it to win it. My awareness was rising. I went back to school to study core stability, chakra balancing, and the fascial system. What I learned changed the trajectory of my entire career.

It seems the inner ear isn't the only boss of my balance. After years of study and practice, I'm now the rock star of stability—mind, body, and spirit.

Revelations

When my hearing loss became known throughout my network, women reached out from far and wide to connect with me.

"Julie, I heard the news. What can I do?"

"Have you tried the Epley maneuver? Acupuncture? Massage?"

"You must be so stressed."

"Is it caused by medication? Ménèire's disease? A neuroma?"

They wanted to hear my story, but I didn't want to tell it. I'd always been a lone wolf, an introvert, very private, and a bit distrustful of women. You see, I was bullied by girls in high school, so my pattern ever since then was to keep my distance and resist being vulnerable for fear of judgment. However, that didn't last long after my hearing loss.

It was the last night of my first women's wellness retreat when I chose to make a change. My priorities were shifting. It was time to be vulnerable. *My heart is racing even now as I write this.* There were eight of us sitting at a long wooden table under a massive Ceiba tree in the Yucatán region of western Mexico. The energy of that evening was beautiful, and I was inspired.

Nonetheless, my inner voice was chattering wildly, warning me to stay silent. *You'll look weak, Julie. How will they react? Don't share too much, and please, whatever you do, don't get emotional.* I felt the fear and noticed the shame, yet shared my hidden truth anyway.

"Follow your intuition and do what *feels* right to you. Not what you *think* is right." – Alexa Carlin. (4)

Those women chose to follow me on retreat as their guide and teacher, and I deeply felt their trust. Sharing some of my innermost thoughts and feelings with them actually changed my life.

It didn't fix the hearing in my right ear. It's even better than that: now I can be vulnerable without fear of judgment.

Ever since that evening under the Ceiba tree, the highlight of all my retreats is when we connect with ourselves and each other by sharing our stories. This is truly how my instability shifted from a blessing to a curse—not just for me but also for them. My revelations encouraged other women to then reveal their own issues with life balance, body stability, and the causes behind their shame. Most claimed they were disconnected from their own needs and felt weak in their core. I had to know more.

In the following weeks, my research revealed a shocking number of women struggling with symptoms related to the stability muscles of their core and pelvic floor—leakage, pain, pressure, urge, and frequency. It seemed that not only were they struggling physically, but their mental, emotional, and sexual stability was affected, as well. *It's all connected.* This made sense to me. The fact that these issues were affecting them in more ways than one was logical and obviously quite tragic. I simply *had* to help them.

Priorities as a Practice

Have you ever said the following sentence or heard someone say it? "Don't make me laugh; I'm gonna pee my pants!"

We joke about it; then, we typically change the subject. Oh, the shame surrounding this topic! But *why*? Let that shame shit go, sister. It's not serving you.

If you feel embarrassed to speak of these issues to your friends, partners, and doctors, you may spend your life thinking these issues are normal. They're incredibly common, but that does *not* mean they're normal. It means it's time for you to share.

Wait until you hear about this one time. In short, I'll say this: Cassie trusted me with her truth.

"If we can share our story with someone who responds with empathy and understanding, shame can't survive." – Brené Brown (5)

You know when you can feel someone's energy, and it makes you want to cry? This is how it happened, and what she said rocked my entire world.

There were fourteen women at my yoga workshop, we had just wrapped up, and some were still rolling up their mats.

Because yoga isn't limited to physical poses, we ended with a relaxation technique, so we were all feeling grounded and groovy. The music still played softly, the lights were low, and the space felt still and safe. I saw her coming, and the closer she got, the more I felt her anxious energy. I opened my arms and took her into a hug.

She whispered, "I leak when I laugh, so I just stopped laughing."

Uhh. Oh my goodness. What do I say? I said nothing, yet felt everything. *How can I help? What do I do?* I just held her and deepened my breath.

"You're the first person I've told."

When she heard she wasn't alone in her struggle, she smiled. *Yesss, she's feeling hopeful.*

"And I'm not prioritizing myself because I'm taking care of everyone else!"

"I get it. Love, compassion, priorities, and duty, but what about *you?*"

Cassie revealed she'd been struggling with symptoms for eleven years. During that entire time, she was mired in guilt and shame. She resented her body for changing and was sad that she'd not made herself a priority sooner. She felt unstable in so many ways.

In my work, this is what we all have in common. When we hold imbalance or instability in one way, we hold it in another. Instability may begin in one space, then it typically shifts. True story! Listen to your body when she whispers because you don't want to hear her scream. This is precisely why I've made my body as important as my business. My to-do list includes everything from *releasing the clenching in your jaw* to *practicing your speech* to *painting your toenails.*

Again, we're physical, mental, emotional, sexual, spiritual, and energetic human beings. It's all connected. And in case you haven't heard, this is pretty much the definition of yoga. The ancient word *yug* actually means union—mind, body, and spirit. Essentially, it means *you connecting with you.*

Tough Love Talk

To be frank, I still have trouble with self-connection when sharing my truth. I'm often scared shitless! *How will I be judged? Am I good enough? Will they even like me?* Noticing your inner voice and redirecting your thoughts may be your most beneficial practice ever. Neuroplasticity is your capacity to change dysfunctional thinking. (6) Most importantly, be mindful enough to notice, then simply redirect your thoughts.

Yes, I am good enough. They listen because they want to learn. They are rooting for me!

For the record? It's a practice. It took me years to recognize this: Judgment is in the heart of the judge. The fact that I still sometimes feel shame implies I am human, but my dignity does not depend upon your judgment. If your opinion is negative, that's neither here nor there and, frankly, none of my business.

As an inspirational speaker, I weave in my personal stories with purpose. Going to my edge and facing my fears is now part of my work. For the first twelve years of my career, this wasn't the case. I worked like a dog, partied like a professional, and kept my personal life private. It took a health crisis that (quite literally) knocked me over for me to start cultivating my stability. I'm not afraid anymore to admit it.

Listen, eleven years is a long time. I don't want anyone else to wait as long as Cassie did to share her truth. Not one more moment should pass you by without connecting with Self. Perhaps you place your hand on your heart, close your eyes, and simply smile. See? Feels nice, right? There are so many things you can practice every day in some way to experience quick and easy wellness wins. Let me tell you all about them.

THE PRACTICE

Yoga in Real Life

This will be the simplest transformation you've ever experienced. It can start happening today! Important Note: Just because it's simple doesn't mean it's easy. Secret #7 is your key to success.

I'm about to share with you my seven secrets to feeling joyful, stable, and sexy every day in some way. But before I do that, let's back up a bit, shall we?

Way Before the Downward Dog

The first indication of the practice of yoga can be traced back 5,000 years. Yes, that's way before, well, pretty much everything. There were drawings found in caves and transcriptions on palm leaves found in the land that is now known as Northern India. Throughout yoga history, there were four periods of development—Vedic, Pre-Classical, Classical, and Post-Classical.

Here's a quick recap. The yoga teachings during the Vedic Period (~1500BC) produced a number of texts that entailed collections of songs, incantations, and rituals for the sake of transcending the boundaries of the physical mind. When was the last time you transcended the boundaries of *your* physical mind? Sounds impossible, right? Yep, this is why we call it a practice. Then there came the Pre-Classical Period (~500BC), where the teachings focused on self-knowledge, action, and wisdom. In the Classical Period, the first approach was presented in Patanjali's Yoga Sutras (7), written in the second century. It contains the 'eight-limbed path' toward enlightenment. In the Post-Classical Period, a more physical practice was established to cleanse the body and prolong life. This was the period that led to what we now know as Hatha Yoga—the 'yoga of activity'—a posing practice originally developed as a means to warm the body to prepare the nervous system for the stillness of meditation. Fast forward to the late 1800s, when Eastern yoga masters began traveling into the Western world. In the 1920s and 1930s, yoga was strongly promoted, and various schools and organizations began to develop. Then yoga entered mainstream America with a smash in 1947, when Indra Devi opened her studio in Hollywood, California, and gained the devotion of Greta Garbo, Robert Ryan, Elizabeth Arden, and Marilyn Monroe, among many others. Since then, our Western world has seen the development and popularity of many various styles of practice, including (but not limited to) Ashtanga, Iyengar, Kundalini, and Vinyasa.

That all being said, I'd like you to stay focused on *you*. This history is all-encompassing and can be a bit overwhelming. If you recall, the definition of yoga is union—mind, body, and spirit. Everything you need is deep within you. *Whoa. I know.* Stay with me.

The Journey of the Self, Through the Self, To the Self

Secret #1: Be kind to your mind.

I don't know about you, but my mind hops around like a monkey in a tree. It's a rascal and often gets me into trouble. I try to remember *not* to believe everything I think.

One way to be kind to your mind is through a mantra. Meaning "mind tool," a mantra is a sound, word, or phrase that, when repeated, can provide positive transformation. You may repeat it three times or three hundred. The more you practice, the easier and quicker you can redirect your thoughts. Simply notice when your thoughts aren't serving you in a positive way, then keep the mind busy by repeating your mantra.

The mantras I've found most success with are the following:

- I am practicing.
- I feel balanced.
- I am enough.

Secret #2: Listen to your body.

It's more helpful to be proactive than reactive when it comes to your body. I mean, it's just anatomy. Be the boss of your body instead of your body's bitch. Think about it in terms of your car. Please don't wait until you're on the side of the road with no oil in your engine to put more oil in your engine.

Introducing the Sufi Grind: an ancient technique you can practice sitting in a chair or on the floor. In a chair, plant your feet on the floor a bit wider than hip's distance apart, palms down on the thighs, and circle the torso in one direction for ten breaths, then switch directions for ten breaths. Inhale as you lean forward and exhale as you lean back, completing the circle. If you're sitting on the floor, fold your legs in, then switch the fold when you change direction.

Secret #3: Celebrate your Spirit.

Whether you recognize your spirit as a deity, your heart, or your emotions, celebrate your spirit through laughter! This cultivates joy, and according to yoga tradition, we hold our joy in the same region of the body as we hold our shame. With that in mind, consider this: do you prefer weeds or flowers in your garden? Yep, that's what I thought. Cultivate joy!

I'm a certified Laughter Yoga Leader, and we practice laughter at all my workshops, retreats, and even during some of my speeches. Whether fake or real, laughter truly *is* the best medicine. The list of benefits is a mile long.

Grab a girlfriend or your partner, set a timer for one minute, look at each other, no talking, and start to laugh. Continue laughing until the timer sounds. If you feel awkward or uncomfortable, do it anyway. It gets easier once you can move beyond how silly you feel. Hey, there's nothing unhealthy about feeling silly. Are you with me? Hahahaaa!

Secret #4: Remember, it's all connected.

You may be surprised to hear this, but it doesn't take any extra time to practice yoga. Regardless if you roll out a mat or even attend classes, you're already practicing. You're stretching when you're sore, seeking inspiration when you need a second wind, and resting when you're pooped. It's just human nature. You have everything you need; now it's time to be intentional about practicing what you need when you need it.

Secret #5: Contemplate your rituals.

Add to your routine when appropriate and remove negative patterns that no longer serve you. Look at your life. What are your daily rituals in the bedroom, bathroom, office, and kitchen? Recognize when a ritual can be combined with a new practice. Take three deep breaths before getting out of bed, stand on one foot while brushing your teeth, and stretch your back in a hot shower. This is yoga in real life. What an amazing way to begin your day!

Secret #6: Practice makes practice.

Write down your priorities. Where does self-care fall on your list? Is it even *on* your list? If not, put it at the top, please. *Now.* Believe me when I say self-care *isn't* cliché. It's the practice of *you* connecting with *you*, and this is truly of the utmost importance for your well-being.

Secret #7: Just. Keep. Practicing.

Ignoring your needs and rationalizing your negative patterns doesn't serve you one bit. How do I know this? Been there, done that! I made the shift and am thriving as a result. My perspective now comes from a place of empowerment, my health has improved, and my career has catapulted.

You can do this too, sister. Along the way, bear in mind you're not just a bunch of bones and organs in a skin suit. You're a physical, mental, emotional, sexual, spiritual, energetic badass, so put on your big girl panties, keep practicing, and get ready to rock your own world!

For more poses, breath work, and techniques specific to pelvic floor wellness, chakra balancing, fascia, and much more, join the Yoga In Real Life membership here: https://www.stretchyourspirit.com/yogainreallife

References:

1. Idiopathic definition: https://www.vocabulary.com
2. Take the Lead, by AliceAnne Loftus

3. Mayo Clinic:
   https://www.mayoclinic.org/healthy-lifestyle/consumer-health/in-depth/mindfulness-exercises/art-20046356
4. Adaptable: How to Lead with Curiosity, Pivot with Purpose, and Thrive through Change, by Alexa Carlin
5. Daring Greatly: How the Courage to Be Vulnerable Transforms the Way We Live, Love, Parent, and Lead, by Brené Brown
6. Neuroplasticity, Psychology Today:
   https://www.psychologytoday.com/us/basics/neuroplasticity
7. Patanjali's Yoga Sutras:
   https://yogajala.com/the-yoga-sutras-of-patanjali-a-guide/

Obsessed with cartwheels and alone time, Julie Blamphin is a yoga pro, inspirational speaker, retreat leader, and the founder of Stretch Your Spirit.

Known for her positive vibe and racy authenticity, Julie inspires women to feel joyful, stable, and sexy through movement and stillness. Her programs, retreats, speeches, and articles often touch on taboo topics and always highlight hope in healing.

Julie has been featured in AARP The Ethel, Livestrong Magazine, The Leading Lady Podcast, Baltimore Banner, The Dr. Kinney Show, and Pelvic Health Support Canada, among others.

Her teaching approach is a synthesis of Western science and Eastern wisdom. Her experience and education include (but are not limited to) Registered Yoga Teacher Certification (2009), Mindfulness-Based Stress Reduction, Pelvic Floor Yoga with Leslie Howard, Transcendental Meditation, Laughter Yoga, and The MELT Method with Sue Hitzmann.

Julie can whistle like a champ and loves to laugh, dance, travel, and dream in Spanish.

Follow her on Social Media:

https://www.facebook.com/StretchYourSpirit

https://www.instagram.com/stretchyourspirit

https://www.linkedin.com/in/JulieBlamphin/

To book Julie to speak, or learn more about her and her business, visit her website at https://www.stretchyourspirit.com/

Chapter 3

DON'T SETTLE FOR NO

Tearing Through Red Tape with Creative Problem Solving

Lisa M. Van Wormer, Government Contracting Consultant

MY STORY

"Finalists, we are going to take a few minutes to discuss and vote for the winner of the Women Veteran GOVCON Boot Camp Accelerator Pitch Competition."

When the screen went black, and the five of us were transferred to the Zoom waiting room, I grabbed my phone and started texting my husband, Hayden.

H: Pitch session over?
Me: OMG, yes.
H: And?

Me: Went good, I think! I had five minutes to pitch why I should win the $15,000 grant, and then they asked questions for about ten more minutes.

H: $15K!

Me: I know! We could really use it for Abrado.

H: So, what do you think?

Me: I think it's crazy that I'm a finalist!

H: Why?

Me: There were like 40 other women veterans in the Boot Camp program! So many with more established businesses than mine.

H: You're not there by accident; you earned that finalist spot.

Me: But still. . .

Me: Oh, I have to go, they're bringing us back to the meeting, eeek!

H: You got this!

This moment was a pivotal moment for my business, Abrado Analytics. Up to this point, Abrado was established in a "trial by fire" sort of way. I never pictured myself as a business owner, but while being whisked back to the active meeting, I felt exactly where I was supposed to be.

It's funny, I feel like my family is full of entrepreneurial energy. My dad is a tinkerer, and growing up, we always had half-taken-apart microwaves and other electronics spread around our basement and garage to Frankenstein into his newest idea. He was obsessed with technology and poured over the newest gadgets trying to convince us how a square piece of plastic that could hold five downloaded songs was the future and would replace CDs and tapes. He was always ahead of his time.

He and my mother instilled in all of us a strong sense of independence, especially with my sister and me, to never let anyone tell us we couldn't do or achieve what we wanted just because we were girls. They encouraged us to forge our own path, be our own boss, and not take any shit from anyone just because they were in charge at the moment. And looking at the four of us well into our forties, I would say we all heard the call, albeit in different ways.

We grew up as some of the first video gamers without even knowing it. We had an Apple II+ and would all race home and argue over who got to play Reading Rabbit, Frogger, or Zork. When I got a turn, one of my favorites was this game where you programmed a face made out of computer characters to sing a song using DOS. I loved getting the creepy face with the expressive eyebrows to sing *Bicycle Built for Two*. We were the first people I knew to have the initial internet, and my mom would make us get off the phone so she could check the message boards to see if the people she was playing Scrabble against had taken their next turn. We grew up on the edge of technology, and I'm still in awe of how far it has come and how far we're going.

My older brother tried to build his own computer pieces when he was around ten years old. My dad would bring him home spare parts, and he took them apart and put them back together for hours on end. He finally built his first computer at 15 so he didn't have to share with anyone and turned his gaming/computer hobby into a career where he now works in one of the largest technology divisions shepherding, improving, and integrating emerging technology around the globe.

My younger brother became obsessed with the internet, the way it works, the way it processes and catalogs data, and all the ways to harness its power. He has made his home on the cutting edge of all things 'internet' and is a force to be reckoned with in debates on its functionality, ethics, and oversight. He built a consistently evolving business around the newest internet technology, safety, and adaptability, with a heavy focus on social media exploitation. If there is a new app or feature in the public eye, he is the one to call.

My sister, the best athlete of the four of us, focused her energy on health and wellness, bringing to market multiple multi-million-dollar cutting-edge training programs, assessment and monitoring tools, and client-focused healthcare resources utilized by hospitals and employers worldwide. She did this all while making sure she was the smartest person in the room when it came to healthcare reform and policy to consult and drive U.S. policy and private business down the emerging technology-driven healthcare landscape.

All three are so driven by their "it" factor. They found the thing they loved, all as early teenagers, and have made lives and careers surrounding those things. I've always been a bit in awe of their clear vision, and it made me wonder what mine was.

Being number three of four kids in a very loud and outgoing Italian household with a steady stream of neighborhood kids in and out throughout the day can be a daunting and overwhelming existence growing up. But for me, I couldn't get enough. I thrived in the comforting chaos of it all. I learned everyone's names, who their siblings were, and even their pets' names. I always rushed when the phone rang and loved keeping tabs on who was calling whom and why, basically, little sister call screening.

"Hey, is your sister there?"

"Who is this?"

"It is Mike."

"Mike who? Mike C.? Mike S.? Mike L.?"

"Uh, no. Mike H."

"Mike H.? Oh, I know you. You play football with my brother. Why are you calling my sister? She's a junior you know, aren't you a freshman?"

"Um, I just wanted to talk to her."

"But why?"

"I, uh. You know. Hey, is she seeing anyone right now?"

It was times like this I reveled in running to my sister and reporting back on how my brother's friends were going to try and ask her out. I always felt energized when the house was full and loud, and I constantly asked questions and tried to know and hang out with all the different groups of friends that came over, much to my siblings' annoyance at times.

Sure, I had traditional middle-child people-pleaser vibes, but I now see it was always so much more than that. At a young age, I wanted to be included. I wanted to be in the know. And not as a gossip-collecting bystander; I wanted to be in all the inner circles of trust. I floated in and around all of the groups at school. I made friends, and the ones I found that filled me up, I dove in greedily.

It wasn't good enough to be in the National Honors Society; I had to be the president so I could pick and organize the service events we did. When I was on the student council, I loved keeping everything running smoothly. I made sure all the proper forms were filled out and teachers were notified on time, so I could champion events I wanted and make new activities and dances throughout the year, knowing I built enough goodwill and understanding of the system to push them through. On the swim team, the competitive monster inside me made sure I was one of the top butterfliers on the team, but I needed more. I wanted to assist the coach, help manage the practice, pick the swimsuit designs, help organize our banquets, pick out the trophies, and even went as far as creating award categories so each swimmer was recognized at the end of the season for something unique about them and their contribution to the team.

The quest for a say and influence followed me my whole life, and it wasn't until I was in the U.S. Army, one of the most rigid systems created, that I truly found my footing as a professional change-maker and creative problem solver.

When considering joining the military, one of the most common things I heard was, "I could never because I hate being told what to do." Yes, that 100% exists in the military, like all of the time. My dad, also a former Army soldier, *hates* being told what to do, and yet he volunteered for four tours during the Vietnam War because, to him, doing what was right was more important than hating being yelled at. So, as a result, to complement the strong independent streak and a love for technology, he definitely gave all four of us a huge chunk of the chip on his shoulder when it came to being told what to do.

Let me be clear, I also *hate* being told what to do, especially in scenarios where I'm expected to shut up and do what they say or when it's used as a tool to stop me from accomplishing something. Before joining the Army, I did try to convince people to let me do what I wanted in the way I wanted, almost as a personal quest in life, it seemed. I wonder how rich my parent would be if they had a dollar for every time I asked, "But why?" I wanted to know not just what the rule was but why it existed. Even back then, I knew understanding why a rule, limit, or restriction was in place was the first step in getting around it. But I didn't really have the tools or confidence to push through the people-pleaser pressure and make waves. Though I never shied away from calling someone out for being mean or a bully and mistreating someone, I struggled with the awkwardness of trying to convince someone to do what I wanted. It was my time in the Army that really unleashed my superpower.

Basic training is awful, even if you like running. It's literally an exercise of infinite patience. The hurry-up-and-wait culture of being so ridiculously early to an activity time so you can sit around and wait silently in formation, sometimes for hours, for someone to show up and tell you it's time to walk to the chow hall to eat is maddening. The rigid structure wasn't the problem for me. I thrive in structure. Structure, to me, is understanding the box someone wants me to live in. Once I understand its dimensions, then I can pull out my own tape and remold the box to the shape I think works best.

Some Army recruits start to lose it on day one; they question their decision to even join the Army and start pushing boundaries and acting out. I watched how the Drill Sergeants reacted to these pushes. One morning, about three days into orientation (meaning we hadn't even made it to our basic training company yet), one girl decided she didn't feel like getting out of bed.

"No one is even here yet. I'm not getting up just because some guy is going to be here in an hour to tell us to wait another hour before we can rush to the chow hall and be forced to eat breakfast in under seven minutes."

I totally understood, and she was right. But after she called the rest of us idiots and rolled back over and pulled the scratchy green blanket back over her head, I knew she was making a choice that would turn out badly for her. And, as predicted, it did. When the Drill Sergeant saw her missing, found her still in bed, and began yelling, she doubled down and yelled back. While I admire a good double down, I saw no gain for her. We all stood in formation and watched her doing push-ups while she was screamed at by five Drill Sergeants as they circled her like sharks for what seemed like an hour. While I understood her frustration, I couldn't see any gain in her bucking the system in that way. After all was said and done, we ended up being late for breakfast that morning and only got three minutes to shovel food down before we all went on an unplanned four-mile run.

However, about three weeks later, we were assigned KP duty, which is where you have to do chow hall clean-up and dishes for the whole day. It seemed reasonable that each group had to do it at least once, but this would be our second time in a week, and that didn't seem normal. I watched our Drill Sergeants talking about it right before formation, and I could feel that they were just as pissed about the situation as we were all about to be.

And this is one of those moments.

One of the moments where paying attention gives you a glimmer of the edges of the box.

"2nd Platoon has KP duty again today. Shut your mouths and fall in. I need three volunteers to lead the group and…"

My hand shot up. The Drill Sergeant looked at me and said to the group, "See. We have at least one soldier who knows how to suck it up and do what needs to be done."

After leading the march to the chow hall, I immediately volunteered for the worst role on KP, running the door. It was hours of standing up and counting people in and out while watching other soldiers get screamed at as they fidgeted in line, waiting to go into the chow hall. It sucked, just as expected. But, toward the end of the four-hour shift, my Drill Sergeant warmed a bit toward me, and we even had a tiny regular human conversation about where I was from and how long he had been in the Army. That night I was called out of formation and thanked publicly for stepping up. And after formation, I was given fifteen extra minutes of phone time as a reward.

After that day, I saw my way through the suck of Basic Training. Volunteer for the things that no one wants to do and be the person who steps in and does the task without complaining.

The reliable one lives on the edge of the box and gets to see how it's put together. It was the missing piece for me—building that goodwill bank to earn the influence I desperately wanted. I'm not suggesting doing things you're uncomfortable with, but we all know someone has to do the dishes in the house. Otherwise, the kitchen smells, and you get fruit flies everywhere. Consider being the one who takes on the full sink of smelly, food-encrusted dishes everyone is avoiding. Yes, it'll be gross, but it could mean that down the line, you get a free pass on future dish rotations.

Being the reliable one and the trusted team member has paid major dividends throughout my career and my life. When I hated doing land navigation courses in the thick of the woods on the same course for the last decade, I volunteered to create a new one that went around the whole post instead and was more of a historical scavenger hunt. When I wasn't feeling super successful as a linguist in the Army, I took on leadership roles as an analyst in the office to connect dots across all of the hard work that better linguists than I were doing. When the Army stopped feeling like a home for me, I found jobs that used my skill sets in a different way and became a government contractor. When my contracting job lacked the influence to move projects forward— that I had dedicated years of my life to—I adapted and found positions I could mold and flex into the best use of my unique talents. I kept up my spirits and energy and navigated across government contracting spheres to find fits for me and build jobs and projects that filled me up in some way.

And my dad's advice kept bouncing around in my brain—I could do this my own way on my own terms. Instead of moving around and finding the right work with the right influence, I could try this on my own terms. After a decade of being the go-to person for certain tasks and a trusted and reliable team member, I put out feelers.

If I build my own company, will there be a place for me? What if I could take this work that is hard to hire for off of your hands?

Knowing the business and having the connections let me truly see the holes, the places no one was stepping up to do. Looking at those holes to find the ones where I could do the most good and be most successful is where Abrado began. Reading a room, project, or potential business relationship and seeing not only where I fit but where I will thrive is my superpower. It led me to find amazing companies to work with and quickly see which ones weren't worth the effort to continue. It helped me build a bottom line of what is tolerable and pathways to make the tolerable lead to new and exciting opportunities, all while having the infinite patience to wait through the suck.

I also refuse to accept "no" as an answer to something I really want unless I've heard it at least three times. And even then, it's all about reframing the question, figuring out why they're saying no and if they actually have the authority to do so, and then charging ahead to convince them that what I want is what we all want and need.

Paying attention led me to build Abrado as a woman-owned and service-disabled veteran-owned small business. I found my niche not just as the reliable one but now as a set-aside contracting partner. In government contracting, a certain amount of contract dollars must be awarded to set-aside businesses. My vision for Abrado isn't to own and manage government contracts with hundreds of employees. I've always seen the path of Abrado as being a clutch team member, one who does their job extremely well and helps the larger team succeed. Paying attention to where I fit best led me to AliceAnne's Masterclass, where I cemented in my business model that not every dollar is a good dollar, and finding Abrado's best business fit was the key to me finding happiness and fulfillment as a business owner. I learned there is no one path to becoming a business owner and that I could take all the skillsets and unique lessons learned and use those to embolden Abrado down its success trajectory.

And paying attention led me to register for the Women Veteran GOVCON Boot Camp Accelerator 6-month Masterclass and its culminating Pitch Competition. I knew who I was, what I wanted Abrado to be, and where I planned to take it to thrive.

As my computer screen went black and I was brought back into the live Pitch Competition results meeting, I knew being a finalist was proof I was on the right track. It didn't matter how non-traditional my path was; I was still here among other amazing women who forged their own ways to build businesses that drove their careers, their families, and their lives on the path they chose.

"Welcome back everyone, and without further ado, let's announce our winners."

They read out who won third place, and we all clapped as she said her thanks to the committee. As they started to say who won second place in the competition, Zoom stalled again. I just rolled my eyes and waited; it was like this the whole call today. When everything refreshed, I heard, "Congratulations Lisa."

Wait, who? I unmuted myself.

"I'm sorry, it cut out again. Did you say, Lisa?"

I grabbed my phone and started texting Hayden.

> Me: I think I won second!
> H: You think?
> Me: Well, Zoom froze again, ugh!
> H: So annoying.
> Me: Wait, hold on.

"Lisa. Are you back?"

"Yes, sorry. I am back!"

"Well, we were really impressed with your pitch and all of your hard work throughout this Masterclass."

> Me: Um, I think I won. . .
> H: Wait, really?

I still wasn't sure if I had won or if I was being thanked for just being a finalist. So, I said, "It has been such a great experience for me; I have learned so much."

"It is our pleasure to award you $15,000 to help move Abrado forward through what we know will be a successful career. . ."

> Me: I WON!
> H: WOW! I knew you could do it!

THE PRACTICE

Spoiler Alert: There is no checklist to success

Here is what I wish I could offer you. I wish I could deliver you the "Checklist for Success." The thing is, it just doesn't exist. It depends on too much. And I get it, "it depends" is big and daunting, but don't let it overwhelm you. We may not have the one checklist that rules them all, but here are some fundamental questions to ask yourself that can help you build the path for your vision.

I started Abrado Analytics with a vision of continuing to support the people and missions from when I was in the Army. Okay, but what does that look like? I looked at the things I was uniquely good at, where I really shined, and started coming up with ways to take my zone of excellence to market. Perfect, now I have an idea of my niche and my clients, but what does my owning the company bring to the table? This was the tough question. It took me a while to really delve down into what my core values were and find out what success meant to me. This is such an important exercise that will help you find the right direction for your business and for your life. In my head, I had this idea of what "Business Owner Lisa" needed to be, benchmarks of success, influence, money, cars, houses, etc. But when I took the time to truly consider what I wanted to get out of my life and how being a business owner could support me in reaching those goals within my values, "Business Owner Lisa" looked a lot different. So, take the time to really figure this part out. Find a coach that is right for you, like AliceAnne is for me. Find the place, space, and time to be mindful of what you want to build so that when you get there, you are happy and fulfilled.

Find Your Way in and Fight to Stay There

Another checklist that does not exist is "How to Become a Government Contractor." Boy, do I wish it did! Government contracting dollars account for billions of the government's budget across the U.S. alone each year. You'd think that means there's enough for everyone to get some, and in theory, that's the idea. But in practice, those dollars are dressed up in so much red tape you could spend years planning and trying to find your footing just to keep your business afloat. And then you could be right at the finish line, and a project gets squashed at the last minute for who knows why, and the truth is you may never find out. Maybe a war broke out on the other side of the globe, and your project's earmarked funding was diverted to assist in the safety and security in that area. Maybe the contracting officer in charge had a little too much fun, and when what happened in Vegas didn't stay in Vegas, he was removed from his position, and all his in-progress projects got canceled. Dollars get moved, and projects get changed or canceled every day. This happens to everyone in the government contracting realm, insiders and newbies. The fickleness of the promise of government dollars adds such a complicated layer to building and maintaining a successful business.

But don't let that deter you if this is the path you want to choose. For me, it's always about mission. Being in and around the military community has driven my career choices for over twenty years. I've tried to leave the Intelligence Community, but nothing else is as fulfilling to me as supporting the most vulnerable assets when they need it most. I've helped bring products to soldiers in the field that literally save lives, and I feel compelled to continue this path because I've been the one out in the sandbox feeling the weight of impossible tasks, and I was so grateful when I was using a computer or system that didn't break, or had a tool with technical documentation that actually helped, or even had people who cared enough to fly out to a war zone and fix their product so we could continue with our mission. Find the area where your business is the most impactful in the ways most important to you.

We Can All Win Together

When you know who you want to serve and the way you want to do it, getting going is next up. So here is where that non-existent "How to Become a Government Contractor" would be amazing. But since that doesn't exist, here is what works for me.

I had two tools that helped me figure out how to construct the business and find opportunities to go after—Google and my contacts list. I had the benefit of already being in the industry with a small-but-loyal network of friends I could call, ask questions, and pick their brains over happy hour margaritas. And to me, that is the way it should be. The information needed to get started can be so guarded, and I think the reason is that most of the high-value and long-term contracting dollars are competitively bid. This makes sense from the government's perspective to find the best value contractor, but it's a major deterrent in building a supportive, non-competitive government contracting community. It breeds a community that squirrels away best practices and lessons learned and only offers support as long as it doesn't compete with their dollars or opportunities.

And it's immensely frustrating that this serves as a barrier to entry for small businesses in this industry. So frustrating, in fact, that I've made a new mission for Abrado. I want to help people find their footing in government contracting.

This dog-eat-dog, winner-take-all, the-way-it-has-always-been mentality is tired, and we can break the cycle together. Let's get together and find your company's best fit in the government contracting space. We can look at your vision and values and find where your zone of genius has contracting dollars on the table for the taking. Let's strategize together and make attack strategies for your best-fit opportunities and create plans to win these dollars. Let's get you to a win and get your company into the government contracting space. There is enough room for all of us to succeed together!

Go to https://www.abradoanalytics.com/ to learn more!

Lisa M. Van Wormer is an Army veteran and the Owner of Abrado Analytics, a solutions-focused woman and veteran-owned small business dedicated to infusing creativity and innovation into mission success. She has dedicated her life to supporting the missions and the people who continue to put their lives on the line to protect our freedoms and way of life, both through her business and her writing. She loves to support new and leading-edge projects leading them from idea to market, and is always ready to jump on a new challenge with a creative attack strategy.

A lifelong learner, Lisa has a Master's degree in Negotiation, Conflict Resolution, and Peacebuilding from California State University Dominguez Hills and an MFA in Creative Writing and Publishing Arts from the University of Baltimore. She loves the challenge of a new tool or technology and is a staunch believer that an Android phone is far superior to an iPhone.

Lisa is also a wife and mother who does all she can to support her family, friends, and community. She is a community champion and always makes the time to help someone find their path to success and happiness.

To learn more about or work with Abrado Analytics, go to www.abradoanalytics.com or email Lisa at lisa@abradoanalytics.com

To follow Lisa's writing projects and events, go to her professional page at https://www.lmvanwormer.com/

Chapter 4

MAKE YOUR BUSINESS SHINE WITH THE RIGHT GRAPHIC DESIGN

How to Create Powerful Magnetic Marketing Materials that Boost Your Business

Jennifer Osterhouse, Graphic Design Expert

"There are three responses to a piece of design—yes, no, and WOW! Wow is the one to aim for."
~ Milton Glaser

MY STORY

I heard the frustration and tenseness in her voice as I listened to my client talk about her brochure dilemma. "I'm absolutely dreading the upcoming event I'm attending in a few weeks. I was so excited when I signed up for it, but as it gets closer, I really don't want to go. I need an impactful brochure that highlights my nutrition business and includes my branding, the services I offer, and my contact information. I have been agonizing for hours staring at my computer screen. I'm trying to come up with something even remotely professional-looking and just can't make it work. I know exactly what I want the brochure to look like in my head, but I'm struggling to create it."

After talking extensively with my client about her vision for the brochure, we mapped out a design plan and timeline for the project to meet her event deadline. At the end of the phone call, I heard her breathe a huge sigh of relief and knew a weight was lifted off her shoulders. The project was in my hands now. I was tasked with designing an impactful brochure that would make my client feel confident about promoting her business at the upcoming event and also be powerful enough to engage new clients.

Does this scenario sound familiar? Have you spent hours, or even days, spinning your wheels trying to create marketing pieces for your business? Ones that are powerful enough to attract the right clients and boost your profits?

The right graphic design is the key to making your marketing materials shine, and it all starts with a graphic design expert.

The year was 1990, and I was a sophomore at a small college in Philadelphia taking an Introduction to Design class for my fashion design major. I worked on a semester-long project of creating a book about famous fashion designer Christian Lacroix.

I remember I chose him because he was a cool French fashion designer who designed elaborate, brightly colored clothing and handbags. The second part of my project was to create a 3-D item that coordinated with my book. I chose to create an orange silk cylindrical handbag that had colored crystal-like glass beads dangling from the shiny gold trim at the bottom. "Christian Lacroix" was written at an angle using a smooth puffy paint pen inside the lining of the bag. The words were repeated multiple times, creating a pattern in bright hues of orange, blue, green, and hot pink, and a gold-beaded drawstring was the final touch to pull the handbag together.

I loved working on the layout and design of my book. I remember sitting in my dorm room diligently tapping away at the keys on my electric typewriter, *click, click, click,* as I wrote the copy. I wanted to add some unique visual interest and texture that popped off the pages. I decided to use a special colored art paper that had a smooth surface with beautiful, vivid, saturated color on one side and plain white on the other side. I spent an abundant amount of time paying attention to the details of my book design—how each page was laid out, the size and placement of each image, how the copy flowed, and the color-coding of the chapters using the colored art paper to coordinate with my 3-D silk handbag. I was so inspired by the process of creating this book that I wanted to know more about it. I went to my professor and asked, "What is making this book considered? Does this exist as a potential career?" She said, "Absolutely, it's considered graphic design." Right then and there, I knew I found my true passion. I switched colleges, changed my major to Communication Arts (visual track), and worked hard to earn a bachelor's degree and start my career as a graphic designer.

My career path led me to several creative and innovative graphic design jobs. I had a great mentorship with one of my design professors. She owned a small graphic design studio and hired me right after graduation to assist her with design projects. After working there for a few years, I moved on to a publication company working as a junior designer. I was lucky enough to work with a wonderfully talented art director designing stunning page layouts for three different magazines. I then had the opportunity to work at a mid-size direct mail marketing company as a senior designer. I designed strong, response-boosting promotional health and wealth marketing packages, and this is where it all fell into place. I had a variety of design experiences from those jobs under my belt and decided it was time to take a leap of faith to start my own graphic design business. I was both excited and nervous all at the same time. It was the riskiest decision I ever made, but it worked out beautifully.

For over 25 years, I've been designing impactful marketing materials for hundreds of clients. I'm passionate about designing, and I know from experience that graphic design matters in your business. I recently visited a quaint little wine and cheese shop near the waterfront with a friend of mine. As I walked through the white garden gate and entered the outdoor courtyard, I remembered thinking *I love the logo on their sign; it's so simple yet elegant looking and perfectly branded for a wine and cheese shop.* When I stepped inside the shop and looked around, all I could think was *oh wow, this is so cool.* Their beautiful logo was hanging on a large rustic wooden sign above a glass display case that was filled with fresh homemade bread and artisan cheeses. The attractively designed menus, business cards, and brochures were arranged on top of the marble counter for customers to peruse. And the décor throughout the shop matched the look and feel of their branding to a tee. We walked over to the bread and cheese counter, and my friend introduced me to the owner. I was so excited to meet and share with him how much I loved his logo and the marketing materials he had established for his shop. After having an engaging conversation, he gave me some bread and cheese to take home in a beautiful box with a sticker adorning the top that had the logo and branded colors on it. As I was leaving the shop, I thought, *this is exactly why I pour all my design and marketing expertise into every piece I design. I want my clients to shine.* You know the saying, "A picture is worth a thousand words?" Just like the marketing materials I admired at this wine and cheese shop, expertly designed marketing pieces matter and can be worth hundreds or even thousands of sales for your business.

I love quotes and have a lot of them posted on bright, colorful sticky notes all over my office. One of my favorite quotes is by Milton Glaser, a famous graphic designer. He said, "There are three responses to a piece of design—yes, no, and WOW! Wow is the one to aim for." The right graphic design for marketing materials is paramount to grab the attention of your target client and wow them from the very first glance. Some examples I've seen of the wow factor include an advertisement with a large, compelling image that captures your attention right away, the cover of a magazine with a big, bold, bright-colored masthead or headline that draws you in, a brochure that has a unique format and dynamic design that carries you through the layout, and a social media graphic with a clean and simple look delivering a powerful message. We're inundated with print and digital marketing pieces every day. It's more important now than ever before for your business to stand out. Everyone is distracted by the multitude of ways to communicate, so your marketing materials need to cut through the noise. They need to be impactful and expertly designed with eye-catching visual elements creating the wow factor that will immediately capture the attention of your client and stick with them.

I worked with my client who was struggling with designing a brochure for her nutrition business, tweaking the brochure layout until we got it just right. The design was eye-catching, informative, and persuasive, with the wow factor it needed to attract the right clients to her business. She was so excited when we finished the project and sent me this testimonial:

"I hired Jennifer to help me create a professional service offered marketing brochure for an upcoming event. As a relatively new business owner, this was a first, and the notion of it seemed overwhelming. Jennifer took time and great care in getting to know me and my unique business while giving me concrete and manageable steps to take this task from concept to creation in just a few days. Working with Jennifer was not only easy and enjoyable (even on a tight timeline!), but her patience in ensuring that the finished product was an authentic and accurate reflection of me and my philosophy as an integrative healthcare provider really stood out. Jennifer understood and appreciated the importance of each component of the brochure, down to the tiniest details, patiently working with me until we both felt like we nailed it. The result was a finished product that surpassed my expectations, and in fact, created such enthusiasm in me that I couldn't wait to show it off at an upcoming event!" -P.W.

I love working with clients to strategize ways to maximize the impact of their marketing materials through graphic design. The best place to start is by assessing the marketing materials you currently use for your business to determine if they're working effectively. Are they branded to your established business identity? Are they attracting the right clients? Are they designed in a user-friendly way? Are they consistent and cohesive looking? Is the call-to-action clear and concise? I'll share with you the answers to these questions now so you can assess your marketing materials and uplevel them to their fullest potential. Just like my brochure client, I want you to feel confident about promoting your business with expertly designed pieces powerful enough to attract the right clients to boost your business.

THE PRACTICE

Every business needs both print and digital marketing materials. The right graphic design can help you gain the visibility your business needs to engage the right clients and boost your profits. Assessing your marketing materials will help you to analyze how the design is working and what can be improved to make it more impactful and effective.

I recommend that you gather all your marketing materials, spread them out on your desk, and have them up on your computer screen (for digital media). This will give you an overview of all the marketing pieces you're currently using to promote your business. As you look at everything together, a few things will probably jump out at you right away. But let's get down to the nitty-gritty of assessing your pieces through the lens of a graphic design expert.

Here are five ways to assess your marketing materials to determine if they're working to their fullest potential for your business.

1. Clear and Effective Brand Identity

Are your marketing materials branded to your business identity? Every business should have an established brand. Brand identity is your logo, colors, fonts, and image styles created uniquely for your business. Brand guidelines are typically provided to guide you on how to use your branding properly when creating all your marketing materials. It's essential to follow these brand guidelines so there is a cohesive look and feel to all your pieces. Clear and effective branding helps to build brand awareness and trust with your client.

2. Eye Catching Visuals to Attract and Engage the Right Clients

Are you attracting the right clients to your business? There is a science behind the layout and design of a marketing piece to make it visually eye-catching. When you look at a marketing piece, your eye is going to land on specific elements that stand out in the layout. The headline, images, offer, and call-to-action are key elements. The headline needs to be compelling to draw you in, and the images need to be eye-catching to engage you. If you're selling a product, a high-quality photo showcasing it should be prominent in the layout. The offer and the call-to-action need to stand out so the client can easily respond to you. All these key elements must work together to create a visually powerful marketing piece that will catch the attention of the right client for your business.

3. Intuitive and User-Friendly Marketing Materials

Are your marketing materials designed in a user-friendly way?

The design of your marketing materials needs to be easy for the client to use, read and respond to. The phone number, web address, email address, and QR code need to be clear and concise. For digital media, the web and email addresses need to have active, clickable links that work at the push of a button. The QR code artwork should be crisp and clean looking and, when activated, take you directly to the web or offer page quickly and efficiently. Testing all forms of response on your marketing materials is highly recommended to confirm they are all working correctly. The format of the marketing piece needs to be user-friendly, whether it's a printed brochure that you're flipping through with your hands or a digital graphic that you are interacting with on screen. The easier it is for the client to use and respond to your marketing piece, the more successful it is going to be for your business.

4. Consistent and Cohesive Marketing Materials

Are all your marketing materials consistent and cohesive looking? Just like the branding, all your marketing pieces need to have an established look and feel. Combining the usage of the fonts, logo, and colors along with the style of the images and the treatment of the design will create a consistent look. You want to be able to connect to your client in a variety of ways with a mix of both print materials and digital media. Keeping everything consistent and cohesive looking will visually establish your branded marketing materials with the client.

5. Clear and Concise Call-to-Action on Your Marketing Materials

Is the call-to-action clear and concise? The call-to-action is the element on your marketing materials that prompts the client to respond. There are key elements to your call-to-action that can evoke the most effective response. The copy you use and the type of call-to-action you offer are critical to persuading your client to reach out to you. A phone number, web address, QR code, or mail-in response are all forms of call-to-action that can be used individually or together on your marketing piece. A phone number allows the client to set up a call to speak with you directly, which can establish a personal connection from the first contact. A web address will drive the client to your website or offer page, where they'll learn more about your business, offer, or additional products and services you provide. The QR code drives the client to your website or a custom landing page highlighting your specific offer. And finally, the mail-in response, although it seems like the Pony Express days, it's still very relevant. Many clients are going to take the time to read through your marketing piece, fill out the order form, and drop it in the mail. Having a clear and concise call-to-action on your marketing materials is paramount to visually prompt the client to respond to you or your offer.

I recently had a wonderful experience with a client that was so inspiring that it just reinforced why I love helping clients with their graphic design needs for their business. I listened to my client intently as she talked to me about her marketing materials. "I know that I need to improve my marketing materials and want to do an assessment with you. But to be honest, the thought of pulling together all my marketing stuff feels like a daunting task. I am overwhelmed, a bit unorganized, and a little embarrassed. Quite frankly, I'm just not sure I can fully commit."

I assured her that this was the hardest part and that it would be a breeze once she got over the hurdle of gathering everything. She showed up at my office with an overflowing bag full of marketing materials hanging from her right shoulder and a laptop in her left hand. As we spread everything out on the table and began to sift through and organize the marketing pieces, I could see her shoulders start to drop and relax, and her overall demeanor lightened up. We worked through assessing all her print pieces and digital media and even came up with a few ideas to create some impactful new marketing materials to boost her business.

She was thrilled with how smoothly the assessment process went, and when we were done, she said, "I have been needing to do this for a very long time and just didn't feel confident or that I had the time to do it. I can't believe how easy you made this process, and I am so excited to get started on my new marketing pieces. The time we took to go through everything was so worth it. It is going to benefit my business in more ways than I had ever realized. I have learned from this experience that you can overcome what's holding you back, and the payoff for your business is invaluable."

I hope this chapter has inspired you to think about and evaluate how your marketing materials are working for your business. My goal as a graphic design expert is to uplevel your marketing materials to make your business shine with the right graphic design; attracting the right clients is the key to boosting your business.

Jennifer Osterhouse is the owner and graphic design expert of Jennifer Osterhouse Graphic Design. She has over 25 years of experience specializing in the design of powerful, response-boosting, and eye-catching marketing materials. She spent several years working at a top direct mail publishing company before deciding to branch out and start her own graphic design business. Since then, she has never looked back. She has worked with hundreds of clients, helping them uplevel their marketing assets to promote their products and services, boost their profits, and attract the right clients to their business.

Her goal is to make her clients and their business shine by working her magic of creating impactful marketing materials. With her unique design skill set and wealth of direct marketing knowledge, she can combine copy and design with the client's brand aesthetic to make their marketing materials stand out above the rest. She has a keen eye and meticulous attention to detail. She approaches every project with a clean slate so that every marketing piece she designs is unique to her client, their branding, and the goal of the marketing piece for their business. She believes in quality design, clear messaging, and professional standards in every project she does for her clients.

Jennifer is creative through and through, and designing is her absolute passion (has been and always will be). But, when she is not at her computer designing, she enjoys working out, being active outdoors, relaxing on the beach, spending time with her family and friends, or baking her famous Snickerdoodle cookies.

Jennifer loves quotes, and one of her favorites is from Steve Jobs: "Design is not just what it looks like and feels like. Design is how it works."

Connect with Jennifer:

Website: https://jenniferosterhouse.com/

Chapter 5

THE FOUR KEYS TO REDEFINE HUSTLE

How to Let Your Faith Break the Chains of Overachievement

Erin Harrigan, Christian Business Coach for Women

MY STORY

Everyone loves a rags-to-riches story, right? A real fairy tale kind of story where everything works out in the end. Yet, while we know those journeys take time, many of us clamor for overnight success (sometimes sounding a bit like Veruca Salt in Willy Wonka: "I want it now!"). We don't see the behind-the-scenes work that happens because social media is all about the highlight reel, not the bloopers.

Such is the story of an ambitious woman who worked her way out of childhood poverty to the top of her game, so to speak.

From hand-me-down "rags" to the "riches" of an impressive title, a six-figure salary, a big house, and a luxury car, with a beautiful family standing by. This is my story. And it's a different kind of rags-to-riches tale.

I can't remember a time when I wasn't reaching for something better than what I had—striving for one goal, then the next, hungry for recognition and driven by achievement. When I think back over my history, my identity was always tied to what I accomplished, whether it was being the very responsible oldest of four raised by a single mom, the overachieving young woman piling on classes to appear smarter, or the wife and mom taking pride in the "perfect" family portrait. I always defined myself by the worldly definitions of the day: *super mom, boss babe, high achiever.* And that worked well for me when life, business, and income were up. But when things were down, I reeled in self-sabotage: *I'm not working hard enough. Maybe I'm not meant for this work.* Never publicly, of course. Never let them see you sweat.

Does any of this sound familiar to you?

As a recovering driver, striver, and achievement chaser, I jumped on the corporate sales train right after graduation, putting my grit, determination, and tenacity into action, and rose to that magical six-figure threshold by my 30s. I proudly became the primary breadwinner of the family, and over the next decade, the "riches" continued to grow. This could've been the happy ending. But it wasn't.

When my road warrior corporate career left our family running on empty, with my husband and I passing like ships in the night and desperate for quality time over brand name stuff, the entrepreneur bug found me in a network marketing business that seemed like a golden opportunity to turn corporate life into life by design. It seemed simple: follow the steps, put in the work, and success will come. Naturally, I thought, *consider it done. I'm going to hustle and get to the top!* I promptly poured that same hard work into making my side hustle a full-time gig and began climbing a new ladder alongside my corporate one. It seemed to be working well: rank advancements, earning a luxury car, and eventually, when my corporate job downsized me, this entrepreneur gig seemed to give me the freedom I sought. Except that, I continued to work myself ragged in pursuit of "more" and soon ran into a brick wall.

Do you ever feel like you're rolling along in life, then one day you get up, look in the mirror, rub the sleep from your eyes, and think: *this is it? This is what success feels like? Something's missing because I'm empty and burned out.* That's exactly where I found myself in October 2014.

It was a sunny fall day when I looked in the mirror and thought, *this is what I've been hustling for?* Our finances were a mess, our marriage was struggling, and our family time was mostly relegated to events for my business. I felt alone in the struggle, as if there was a black hole sucking up all the recognition, awards, stages, and income, and it was insatiable. I'm reminded of the Talking Heads lyric: "You may ask yourself, 'How did I get here?' And you tell yourself, 'This is not my beautiful house.'"

When others' promises of success did not fulfill me as I expected, I knew there must be something wrong with me. The spiral of mind trash sounded like:

What am I missing?

Do I not want it badly enough?

Am I not working hard enough?

Is there some "crack" in my belief about the business, the products, or myself?

I spent hours on my knees, even face down on the floor, begging God: "Please God, save my business. Bring me the perfect person to help me be promoted to the top level." What I didn't realize at the time was that I was asking Him to bless my efforts, yet I never once asked Him to show me His will. I was only interested in asking Him to bless what I knew was the way to success: more hustle.

That day I knew something had to change—and clearly that something must be me—but I needed someone to tell me how and what to change. Sobbing and in a puddle of tears on my beautiful back porch on that gorgeous fall day, I swallowed my pride and called a business mentor to ask what I was doing wrong and how I could get back on track to building my empire. I call her the Velvet Hammer because she's classy and graceful like velvet, and her truthful words carry the power of a hammer. I was looking for a quick checklist of fix-it actions.

Instead, she gave me a wake-up call in two short sentences:

"Erin, you don't know who you are or whose you are. Do you know Jesus?"

The words made no sense to me.

I was intentional in writing the vision, making the plan and working it, visualizing the outcomes, and speaking them into existence. Everything I did was calculated for the best outcome for my family. I did exactly what the world said would make me successful. Yet, here's what was missing:

Surrender.

Real surrender to the God who knit me together in my mother's womb, who knows the number of hairs on my head, who created me as His workmanship, and predestined me for good works made to impact His kingdom. And the path to Him was through a real relationship with His son who died for me: Jesus.

Instinctively I knew this story. I believed in and prayed to God. But to me, Jesus was this mash-up of the universe, the law of attraction, and a sort of fictional hero. I didn't truly know Him because I hadn't invited Him to be my savior. Why? Because that meant surrendering my self-reliance. It meant giving up my control over everything. It meant sacrificing my way for His. It meant taking my business, income, family, and my possessions off the idol pedestal. And that required no longer seeing my business (or money) as my savior but instead giving Jesus that throne.

Until I looked up from my personal rock bottom and listened to my mentor's words, I hadn't been ready to give up control and the hustle that fueled my adrenaline yet created a not-so-happy ending to my rags-to-riches tale.

You may be ready to stop reading right here because you don't believe in God because of something you've experienced from other humans. You may not even use the word God (not to mention the name Jesus). Still, if you've read to this point, *there is something in my story that rings true or feels like your own story.* Maybe it's simply that you want to know how this story ends. I invite you to keep reading because there is hope here! Whatever you believe, my mess may be the message you've been seeking.

Self-reliance was my superpower, borne out of being that ultra-responsible, independent oldest child, remember? And the idea of surrender— "Let go, let God"—made me think of one thing: laziness.

Yet the idea that I was made on purpose for a purpose and predestined for a path to use my God-given gifts gave me a glimmer of hope. Hearing that I didn't have to carry these burdens alone (wife, super mom, CEO) or do the work alone made me take a deep breath and let my shoulders fall in relief. Learning there was a path to doing life and business with the guidance of the Creator, who knows me better than anyone, sure sounded better than white-knuckling my way through it all. So that day, October 4, 2014, I said yes to giving Him my life. And that changed everything.

> *Therefore, if anyone is in Christ, he is a new creation, the old has passed away; behold, the new has come.*
> (2 Corinthians 5:17)

I was brand new, and that meant my view of everything was new. Over the next four years, as the Lord worked on me, pulling off layer after layer of doing things my way, He taught me a new definition of hustle: His.

According to WordHippo, "hustle" is most often defined as:

Verb: To force or push one's way; To move quickly; To pressure someone into doing something.

Noun: A state of great activity; A willingness to undertake new or risky endeavors; Great, and often showy or disorderly, speed.

Notice that most of these definitions are about being busy, hurried, rushed, aggressive, etc.

Does it seem to you like the world has only embraced the aggressive definitions? It's like a tug-of-war between two extremes: the frantic, aggressive definition of hustle on one end and the recent "anti-hustle" mantras on the other. Here's what Holy Spirit taught me:

The issue isn't the hustle itself. The issue is how we define and pursue it.

When we emulate how Jesus worked, with purpose, intention, a sense of timing, and always seeking His Father's direction, we can *redefine hustle* and operate in the ambition He gave us. By redefining hustle, we rediscover Jesus' unsurpassed peace, calm, and even joy in our work, breaking the chains of overwhelm and overachievement so we can walk out God's assignment with clarity, serenity, and fulfillment.

What I've learned on my journey, and where I see other high-achieving women (faith-led or not) struggle, is when, in our desire to make an impact, we get lost in a spiral of overwhelm, overachievement, and unfulfillment. I picture these struggles as thick, heavy chains, keeping us anchored to the world's definition of success and unable to move forward with the assignment God meant for our businesses. Often it looks like this:

We're overwhelmed by the call to do more, push harder, and control everything.

We're natural overachievers, and we believe overachieving will bring more/better results. Yet we can't catch our breath.

We're unfulfilled because we hang our hope on achieving the next goal, and no matter how much we succeed, it's never enough.

God has a different system for success, and it's what pulled me out of the pit and turned around my life, relationships, and business. For me, it started with giving my life to Jesus and letting Him lead. Out of my growth with Him, He provided me with this four-key framework for redefining hustle to break the chains of overachievement. I know this practice will help you too.

THE PRACTICE

DEFINE: Allow only God to define you, your purpose, and your success.

When our identity and definition of success are tied to the world's measurement and expectations, it's like being a boat in a hurricane. On sunny days, we're out sailing: making progress, achieving goals, kicking butt, and taking names. But on stormy days, we're taking on water, blowing all over the place, and crashing into things. When business is up, we're on top of the world. When business is down, we're face down in the gutter.

As women leaders, we've got to stop letting the world and other people define who we are, whose we are, and what purpose and success mean for us. The answer is to only allow God to define these things! Who better to define us and our success than He who made us and already knows the rest of our story?

DIRECT: Give God the reigns to direct you, your life, and your work.

We're so busy in our busyness that we've practically created a badge for it. It's the overloading of our plates as ambitious women that sabotages the impact we can make for our families, clients, and the world. You've heard it said time and again that you can't pour from an empty pitcher, but we just keep going. I'm not going to lecture you on self-care. Rather, I'm going to give you an action that may sound cliche and overused:

Let go. Let God.

Give Jesus the wheel. (Yes, I know it sounds better coming from Carrie Underwood). This is not permission to do nothing. We have to work faithfully and rest faithfully. However—and this may fly in the face of everything the world has taught you—doing more is not getting you more. Because that "more" is temporal, shifting sands, and ultimately unfulfilling. It's wearing you out, and it feeds your overachievement without nourishing your life. The key is to stop following your own directions and let God direct you.

It means starting your day by asking for guidance: "Whom can I serve today, and how? What do you have in store for me today, Lord?"

It means making your to-do list mission-focused—specific to what'll move your mission forward—and surrendering your control to let God lead. He is your ultimate GPS (I like to think of Him as the Great Positioning Shepherd). Let Him lead you! Let me be clear: I don't hear His voice like some Morgan Freeman character (though that would be so cool). It's more of me asking for wisdom and guidance and then "listening" for a feeling, seeing a person in my mind, or creating a list of actions. This isn't magic. It's having a daily business meeting with my Heavenly Father and listening for His direction.

DISCIPLINE: Put God's definition and direction into action with discipline.

Raise your hand if you're a list maker. If you're like me, you love checking things off the list and even adding completed tasks just so you can check them off. This third key is critical because it's where we put our faith into action through trust. *Trust* is the action of giving movement to our faith. We have a responsibility to show up and take intentional action. Discipline for ambitious women means taking the knowledge of how He defines you, following His direction, and putting it into action.

We can believe in God all day long. But to experience His promise of unsurpassed peace firsthand, we've got to be moving.

Yes, there is risk in that because we'll face challenges, trials, and awful things sometimes. But it's in taking that risk and even experiencing adversity that we get to know His saving grace and the power of redemption.

DEVELOP: Apply the wisdom gained to develop into the entrepreneur He made you to be.

In business, there's a concept called the closed loop, and it means as we're informed, we do the work and learn things along the way, which are fed back into our work, so we get better at what we do each time we do it. This fourth key, develop, is what pulls the other three together to form our closed loop.

We take the knowledge of how He defines us, combined with His direction, and then apply discipline to put this knowledge into action to continually develop. It's how we grow into who He's made us to be and keep growing deeper in our relationship with Him. It's what feeds our knowledge and depth of accepting His definition and direction, so we can put it into action and develop further. Our Lord loves us so much that He is patient with our growth, allowing challenges to teach us to depend solely on Him, and gives us ways to walk this out—our business being one of those ways.

Together these four keys unlock the chains of overachievement, overwhelm, and unfulfillment by opening three doors we all desire in life and business: clarity, serenity, and fulfillment. Let these words sink in, and imagine how it would feel to have them in your life and business. This practice has opened those doors for me and my clients in the following ways:

Clarity: I know who I am, whose I am, what action to take and when, breaking the chains of overachievement. Clarity gives me the freedom to embrace God's redirection from good human plans to God's best plans. For many, this means a shift in industry or business focus and a shift away from self-reliance to new levels of success. The result: a thriving business in harmony with the priorities of life.

Serenity: I am calm, peaceful, and untroubled in running my business, with my priorities in the right order—God, family, then business—breaking the chains of overwhelm. Serenity gives me the unsurpassed peace and calm that shows up in responding (not reacting) to life and business. For many, it means doors opening for new clients and collaborations because of the refreshing air of hope, calm, and integrity in which they're operating.

Fulfillment: I'm filled by God as my portion, regardless of the outcomes. Yes, I work toward goals, and yes, I achieve many. Yet I no longer have that feeling of success never being enough, breaking the chains of unfulfillment. When our fulfillment is no longer connected to the empty promises of the world, we experience deeper joy and contentment in life and business because our joy and contentment are no longer tied to productivity or performance. Ultimate fulfillment is knowing God provides all you need, and that where He guides, He provides because of our trust and obedience (this isn't a name-it-and-claim-it thing)! The ups and downs in business no longer dictate satisfaction, and there is great freedom in that!

If not for the wake-up call of my conversation with the Velvet Hammer, I imagine I'd still be driving, striving, and achievement-chasing, wracked with anxiety about making it all happen, probably divorced and struggling to make ends meet. Or maybe I'd be wildly rich and yet still deeply unfulfilled.

What does all this mean for you? I hope my story and this practice break the chains of overachievement for you by changing how you see your own journey. I hope this practice shows you where you can go when you unchain your identity from the world. I hope you see that escaping overwhelm, overachievement, and unfulfillment in your life and business is possible. Because the truth is, God has a different definition of success, and He's waiting for you to embrace and align with His great plan for your life.

You may wonder, with the gift of hindsight, if there's anything I'd change about my former driver, striver, and achievement-chaser life, or if there's anything I regret about those years (decades really) I spent in overwhelm, overachievement, and unfulfillment. My answer is a bit of yes and no.

First, there is nothing I'd change about my former approach to life and business. Looking back now, I realize every decision made and every action taken was necessary for God to position me for renewal, redemption, and redirection. Without my past, I'd never have experienced the darkness, isolation, disappointment, and lessons that led me to realize He was the only way out. Those struggles revealed my deep need for a Savior who is steadfast, unwavering, and unfazed by the world's ever-shifting sands. I had to be brought to my knees to look up and discover a deep love and acceptance beyond the temporary high that titles, money, accolades, and possessions provide. Not only to discover His love but to accept it, embrace it, and cling to it in the inevitable future storms.

Secondly, while I have no regrets, here's the hard truth: I still spend time in overwhelm and overachievement, and I won't be "cured" of those struggles on this side of Heaven. Why? Because we live in a fallen world, and that level of "perfection" cannot be found here.

Remember, the world is noisy, distracting, and filled with people doing more and better than you. It's easy for me to overwhelm myself trying to keep up or outdo everyone else. The same goes for overachievement. And if I were "cured" of these struggles and life were perfect, why would I even need Jesus?

The best part is that God made me ambitious, and He gave me a gift for speaking and coaching (aka shepherding/pastoring in terms of spiritual gifts), and my business is one way I administer those gifts. He made me this way to do His work (see Ephesians 2:10), so He already knows what I'm prone to do and think. Thankfully, He's already out ahead of me, preparing the road for overcoming those struggles any time they pop up. And He's given me the tools (the Bible and the four keys framework) to work through them.

One place I've seen remarkable healing is where I seek fulfillment. While I sometimes get caught up thinking that better results, a bigger audience, a longer client list, and a larger bank account would be more fulfilling, those are truly fleeting moments. When those insecurities rear their ugly heads, I recall and rejoice daily over all He's delivered me through, and all He's done far beyond what I could do on my own. I only have to look up at the whiteboard on my office wall to see the list of the promises He's fulfilled and realize they are immeasurably more than I could think or imagine (see Ephesians 3:20)—from saving my marriage to debt freedom to paying cash for college, escaping toxic business partnerships, and more. Most of all, He's led me to find fulfillment in knowing who I am and whose I am. I know that nothing I can do will ever change His love for me.

I'll leave you with one more thing you can apply to your journey right now, and it's something I often ponder.

What if my lifelong runaway ambition, reaching the highest highs and lowest lows of my family, relationships, finances, work, and all the things in between, weren't about success at all? What if all this was purposefully orchestrated by a God who positions us, perfects us, and provides for us? What if it was all about Him moving mountains to show me His will and move me toward His greater plan for my life? I may never know those answers until I get to Heaven (and trust me, I have a long list of questions for my arrival there!). But by allowing Him to define and direct me and putting that into action with discipline, He is gracious to give me glimpses of how the dots connect and how everything develops me. And that is more than enough for me to keep going.

Remember, God made you ambitious. But He didn't make you to do business as usual. Go download your copy of the *4 Keys to Redefine Hustle* at https://erinharrigan.com/4Keys, and put it into practice right away. When you do, you'll realize true freedom!

Erin Harrigan is a Christian wife, empty nest mom, speaker, author, and business coach for high-achieving Christian women who seek to refine or scale their businesses without compromising their faith. Bringing to bear her 30+ years of corporate work and 10+ years of network marketing, she helps women break free from the drain of "business as usual" by aligning business strategy and goals to God's truth. She does this through her customized business coaching, speaking, her award-winning podcast, *Redefining Hustle: Pursuing Success as a Christian Woman*, and her book *Pursuing Success God's Way: A Practical Guide to Hustle with Heart*.

Erin loves the beach, tacos, good cheese, red wine, singing along to Broadway show tunes, and living in Chesapeake Beach, Maryland, with her husband, Brian.

If you're ready to tune out the world, tune into God's truth, and turn up focus to build your thriving business, visit https://erinharrigan.com

Chapter 6

LOVE LETTER TO RESILIENCE

How Sales Mastery Serves as the Gateway to Entrepreneurial Freedom

Michelle Terpstra, Sales Growth Expert

MY STORY

Sales growth isn't a game of chance; it's a relentless pursuit marked by the three Cs: Consistency, Commitment, and Competence.

We all share the same 24 hours a day, no more or less. It's not about the time we have; it's about how we use it. So, let's cut to the chase and focus on fueling our sales growth. Even when everything around you crumbles, you can lean on this to crush your sales goals.

Before we dive into the magic of the three Cs and how you can implement them in your business today, let me share how this simple strategy served me during the most significant transition of my life.

During the summer of 2021, I found myself setting up my new office 3,000 miles away from the sun-kissed beaches of Orange County, California, leaving behind family, friends, and a life we knew for nearly 40 years. We moved to Buffalo, New York, lured by a career opportunity too irresistible for my husband to decline.

It was the hardest decision I've ever made. There were countless sleepless nights, dozens of pros and cons lists, challenging conversations with my family about leaving, giving up my beloved local beaches, saying goodbye to my best friends, and so much more.

As a family, we made the best decision possible and took a leap of faith.

I remember repeating the following affirmation to myself over and over:

Trust yourself, Michelle. Everything is figureoutable. Life is not a linear journey. You will either win or learn. With great risk comes great reward.

Although this was one of my most challenging personal decisions, one thing stayed steady: my business.

Thankfully, running an online coaching and consulting company serving a global clientele afforded me the flexibility to embark on this new adventure without disrupting my work.

Although my heart was heavy, and my mind was a whirlwind of worries—about everything, my kids, our new life, etc.—there was one thing I wasn't concerned about, and that was my sales growth.

One of the greatest business icons in my industry, Marie Forleo, also named by Oprah as a thought leader for the next generation and author of *Everything is Figureoutable*, said, "Success doesn't come from what you occasionally do; it comes from what you do consistently."

Even amidst the chaos of personal transition, I held onto this belief. I was confident I could still meet my sales growth targets, and that's the assurance I want for you each time you face adversity.

Life happens, and it doesn't always play fair. But that doesn't mean your business should take the backseat or suffer.

After working with hundreds of businesses, I know three threads keep them going and growing. If you focus on just these three things, you, too, can get what you want regardless of what comes your way.

Consistency: Business success is very much dependent on repetition and execution. And nothing worthwhile comes without consistent action. Too many businesses fail because of scattered efforts, trying a million tactics without fully committing to any. The secret is to pick one and go all in.

After relocating, I organized a virtual event for launching my business six weeks after my arrival. It helped me focus on my marketing efforts, prioritize clear sales goals, and use my mental resources to settle my family instead of reinventing my client acquisition method.

This recurring launch event was familiar territory; I knew the drill and could execute it without complicating my life even more. The takeaway is to stick to and repeat what you know, especially in times of change and challenge.

Commitment: Life happens, economies fluctuate, and challenges will surface. But if you stay committed, show up daily, and stick to your plan, you won't merely survive; you'll thrive.

Navigating a cross-country move doesn't lend itself to well-laid plans or predictable schedules. I crafted a list of my marketing and sales tasks and fit them into my chaotic day, not the other way around.

The journey wasn't a cakewalk, but commitment becomes the only choice when your passion fuels your endeavors.

It's common for individuals to abandon their goals right before reaching great success because it can be challenging to see the end result when you're fully immersed in the process of building a business. Keep pushing forward, and remember that success takes time.

Recommitting your goals and impact daily, especially in challenging times, will help you see the horizon and keep you motivated to keep moving forward.

Competence: Sales growth demands mastery of sales— no compromises. It's a skill that matures over time. First, you master sales yourself, refine your client acquisition model, and then expand by hiring a sales team.

Consistency and commitment mean very little unless you have the competency to execute.

Competence in this area is the secret sauce to making every action count—sales self-mastery.

Your efforts only matter if you can close the sale. Reading this might feel direct and harsh, but it's the truth that all entrepreneurs need to hear and live by.

I executed my live launch event, but more importantly, I was able to pitch and enroll clients into my program at the end of the event.

Even distracted and consumed by my personal life, I could lean on my sales skills.

And this is why I do what I do.

I know deep down that the more people I teach sales to, the more businesses thrive and the more ideas hit the market—the ripple effect of my efforts at max force.

And that, my friend, is the magic of competence. No matter what life throws at you, you're unstoppable when you've mastered your sales skills.

You have an extraordinary capacity to not just survive, but to thrive.

The three Cs served me, and they can serve you too.

In 2021, amidst the whirlwind of personal changes, I increased sales by over 180% from the prior year.

While the number is impressive, what truly matters is the positive impact I was able to make by helping even more people through my success.

As of mid-2023, my company has served over 1,000 entrepreneurs through our courses, coaching, and consulting, helping them not just survive but thrive.

This love letter to resilience goes beyond just me; I can tell you that my clients have faced and overcome all sorts of personal roadblocks.

They've grappled with cancer scares, grieved over family deaths, struggled with anxiety, and coped with overwhelming life events. They've endured breakups, partnership dissolutions, health and mental challenges involving their children, financial hardship, and even their spouses losing their jobs.

As a coach, consultant, and Fractional Chief Sales Officer, I have mentored my clients during these times to:

- Overcome selling fears.
- Create new offers, products, and services.
- Double their closing rates.
- Make their first high-ticket sale.
- Sell out their group coaching programs.
- Set up sales automation that saves them 40+ hours per month.
- Make the transition from the sales seat and hire their first sales professional.

Each time, they chose resilience just like I did.

If you're reading this and still stuck on the sales is a *too-hard mental loop,* I want to share this with you—I know you will change your tune.

One of my favorite entrepreneurs is Sara Blakely; her grit, creativity, and resilience story is one of my favorites to the top. She is graceful, humble, funny, and wicked smart, but did you know she had her start in one of the most demanding entry-level sales jobs?

She sold fax machines.

Yes, while selling fax machines door-to-door to pay the bills, Sara also created product samples in her kitchen and persistently called on the Neiman Marcus buyer for a meeting.

After months of persistently following up, Sara finally got ten minutes to pitch her invention, Spanx.

A few minutes into the biggest meeting of her life, she was losing the buyer's attention. She asked the perfectly dressed, proper woman to meet her in the restroom. Shocked but compliant, the woman followed Sara. She showed the buyer the magic of the footless pantyhose, and Spanx was born. (source: https://www.npr.org/transcripts/493312213)

Did you know this fun fact about Sara Blakely, the self-made billionaire, and that she started her career in door-to-door sales? This story highlights the importance of the three Cs—consistency, commitment, and competence—in achieving success. Sara's success resulted from her daily actions and unwavering habits, which you can also adopt.

If you've listened to her speak, you know she exudes femininity and is a perfect example of how showing up 100% yourself while selling is the secret to staying in a sales flow.

Part of why I became a sales consultant and mentor is because I wanted to transform the common belief that if you're good at sales (or want to be), that somehow meant that you had to compromise who you are.

It's simply not true. To be your best at sales, you get to be you—your best self. Merely adhere to the 3Cs.

Sara persevered and succeeded, despite initial resistance from the buyer. She used her sales skills and passion to adjust her pitch and hook the buyer. Now, years later, millions of women are enjoying the confidence and comfort of Spanx, thanks to her determination and hard work.

"True fulfillment in life doesn't come from what we get; it comes from what we give." Marie Forleo.

Regardless if you sell pantyhose, supplements, courses, professional services, real estate, or anything, you can make your dreams come true and others as well.

Even during the turmoil in my life moving cross country, what mattered the most was how my methods served my clients, the relationships I made, and the lives I could change. Just like Sara knew women needed Spanx, I know there are endless opportunities for me to help others master sales.

There is a significant difference between mastering a skill yourself and being able to teach it to others. Early in my business, I invested in the knowledge that helped me create robust curriculum and teaching methods to help my clients feel motivated by working with me and confident to take action and implement my strategies.

Hundreds of lessons, worksheets, templates, and scripts have been provided to my clients over the years, and one of my greatest joys is receiving messages from past clients returning to report their ongoing success using my tools for sales growth.

Recently, I got a VOXER message from one of my first clients, saying, "Michelle, it gives me such confidence and safety in my business to know that I have your tools. I use them almost every single day. Even as my business changes, your tools still support me."

So my love letter to resilience is not just about me but everyone around me. Hard times will come and go, but your freedom and growth can flow with it if you dedicate the time and energy to learning the one thing that will get you through anything in business—sales mastery.

I understand that organizing sales systems and using tools effectively can be challenging. That's why I wanted to share my expertise with you. I warmly invite you to check out michelleterpstra.com/resources, where you can access my complimentary tools. Also, I want to let you know that as a reader of this book, you have special access to another tool from me. I hope this all makes your work easier and more efficient.

THE PRACTICE

Achieving success with this productivity tool is within your grasp, but it starts with taking action. You hold the power to set the parameters and make the rules. Let's work together to identify a sales target that's both challenging and attainable, so you can strive towards your goals with confidence.

The key to mastering High-Performance Sales Habits is harnessing the power of the three Cs: Consistency, Commitment, and Competence.

Let's break this down into easy, actionable steps.

Step 1: Select a 90-Day Sales Objective

How do we set a goal that's both ambitious and realistic? Start with understanding your business's current situation and your personal capabilities. Identify the areas where growth can be realized and the resources needed to foster that growth. Your sales objectives could range from generating new leads, enhancing your conversion rates, upselling to existing clients, or expanding your market reach.

For this exercise, let's focus on a specific objective—increasing sales call conversions. But remember, the method applies to any measurable goal.

To select your sales objective, ask yourself:

- What is my current conversion rate on sales calls?
- How much can I realistically improve it in the next 90 days?
- Do I have the resources and capacity to drive this improvement?

Jot down these answers. They'll form the base of your 90-day sales objective.

If you need help analyzing your sales call success and improvements, download my self-assessment worksheet from HighPerformanceSalesHabits.com.

Step 2: Determine the Action Steps

Now, you have a clear objective. But how do you achieve it? By breaking it down into manageable, actionable steps.

List out what needs to be done to reach your goal. Remember, Rome wasn't built in a day, and neither will your sales growth. Patience and persistence are key.

For instance, to increase sales call conversions, your action steps might look like this:

- Improve pre-call planning: Research prospects thoroughly before the call.
- Enhance your sales script: Make it more personalized and engaging.
- Practice objection handling: Prepare responses to common objections.
- Improve follow-up strategies: Implement timely and persuasive follow-ups.
- Conduct or attend regular sales training sessions: For yourself and your team, if applicable.

If you have a team or plan on using freelancers, assign responsibilities for each step. Who's doing what? Clarifying this will prevent confusion down the line.

Step 3: Assign Timelines and Deadlines

With your action steps laid out, it's time to set a timeline. When will each step be started and completed? Keep in mind your steps need to build upon each other logically.

For instance, improving your sales script (Step 2) should follow pre-call planning (Step 1). Conducting regular sales training sessions (Step 3) should probably be an ongoing process starting after the first few steps have been initiated.

Create a timeline that's practical, keeping some buffer for unforeseen delays. Remember, the goal is progress, not perfection.

Step 4: Define Success and Failure for Each Action Step

This is your compass. It helps you understand whether you're moving in the right direction or if it's time to change course. For each action step, define what success and failure would look like.

Take the action step of "improving pre-call planning." Success could mean having comprehensive information about each prospect before the sales call, leading to more personalized conversations. Failure, on the other hand, could look like having insufficient information, leading to a generic sales pitch.

Defining success and failure will serve as benchmarks to assess your performance and make necessary adjustments.

Step 5: Put It Into Action

Congratulations! You've reached an important milestone and are now ready to put your plan into action. Over the next 90 days, focus on completing each action step according to the provided timeline. Remember to check in on your progress regularly and make adjustments as needed. If things don't go as planned, don't worry. The most important thing is to keep learning and moving forward. You've got this!

Bonus: Free Download

I am here to support you every step of the way. To help you on your sales journey, I've put together a sales call assessment worksheet and training that you can access at HighPerformanceSalesHabits.com. This worksheet can help you improve your sales call process, and if you'd like, you can also get a workbook to keep you organized and focused on your sales growth goals.

I encourage you to take the first step, stay committed, and watch your sales soar. I believe in you and your ability to achieve greatness!

Michelle Terpstra is the sales growth expert who makes it rain for startups. She's the author of 'High-Performance Sales Habits,' founder of the Startup Sales Leadership Institute, and a sales maven who's powered over a thousand companies to smash their sales targets.

Michelle's secret sauce? Cultivating killer habits, creating rock-solid sales systems, and molding top-tier sales teams.

Her expertise has seen the spotlight in Shout Out LA!, Thrive Global, Medium, and a long list of premier business-focused podcasts too numerous to count. She's even shared the stage with Chris Voss, the mastermind behind the bestseller "Never Split The Difference."

Michelle's mission with the Startup Sales Leadership Institute is simple but bold: to ignite a sales inferno in every startup, sparking a domino effect of success that resonates beyond each client.

She's not just your consultant; she's your co-pilot in the exhilarating journey of scaling sales. She'll guide you in transforming from a salesperson into a sales leader and from a team builder to a dream builder.

When Michelle's in your corner, you're not just learning the art of selling but mastering the science of leadership and motivation. Friends and clients fondly know her as the hype woman with a master plan, blending digital marketing, social selling, and transforming traditional sales tactics into a potent blend that enhances conversions.

Offstage, Michelle is a beach-lover, party host, travel enthusiast, wine aficionado, and shopaholic. She enjoys hot yoga sessions, rides on her Peloton, and lives for family adventures. With Michelle, it's all about achieving balance, embracing challenges, and, most importantly, having fun on the journey.

Connect with her on the following sites:
https://michelleterpstra.com/
https://michelleterpstra.com/thejournal/
https://michelleterpstra.com/startup-sales-leadership-academy/
LinkedIn: https://www.linkedin.com/in/michellecuocoterpstra/
Facebook: https://www.facebook.com/michelleterpstra/
Instagram: https://www.instagram.com/themichelleterpstra/

Chapter 7

BREAKING THE BURNOUT CYCLE

The Delegation Solution

Chrissy Rey

MY STORY

I can still taste the bitter tang of antibiotics on my tongue as I recall the day I burned out the first time. I suffered from a nasty bout of strep throat that left me bedridden, but the unyielding voice of my boss echoed through my phone, "We need you to come in. We're launching a website today."

Despite my protests about spreading the infection, he insisted I return to the office immediately. His disregard for my health was the wake-up call I needed.

As I dragged myself into the office, hoarse, exhausted, and bedraggled, I couldn't help but question the choices that led me to this point. It was 2001, and I was several years into a fast-paced career as a web developer and technical trainer specializing in Flash. I had a fancy Vice President title and worked on high-profile projects with equally high expectations. I also spent several years speaking at conferences, contributing to books about Flash and web development, and establishing myself as an expert in my field.

At first, the work was empowering, but when I consistently worked twelve-hour workdays for weeks on end, I began to realize the toll it was taking on my well-being. My employers expected me to put my work first and the rest of my life after that. Maybe you can keep that pace for a few weeks or months, but even my body was starting to rebel after years of this. Sure, I made great money, but what's the point of making great money if you don't have time to enjoy the money you make?

That was the day I decided to stop working for someone else. I dragged myself into the office, turned in my laptop, and resigned.

I can do better on my own. I'll just work for myself!

You're probably saying to yourself, "She learned her lesson. I bet the rest of this chapter will be about how working for yourself gives you the flexibility to avoid burnout."

That's what *I* thought, but I didn't realize how wrong I was. I needed to burn out again to learn my lesson. While flexibility is one part of breaking the burnout cycle, much more was required for me.

With renewed resolve, I established myself as a freelance developer, embracing the promise of freedom, flexibility, and control over my workload. After completing a book on Flash that I started writing while still employed, I found freelance clients through my network of colleagues and former students. As the royalties from the book soon replaced about half of my previous salary, and freelance projects more than replaced the rest, I knew I was onto something significant.

I can do this.

As a freshly minted solopreneur, I was eager to prove myself and show the world that I could succeed on my terms. However, while I was the only one responsible for my success, I was also the only one doing the work to provide my core services to clients. I was the lead web developer, designer, and project manager. In addition to handling all of the work related to providing services to my clients, I also had to find clients and convince them to work with me, manage the bookkeeping, send the invoices, do the taxes, and all the other administrative tasks required to support a thriving business. Like many women I know, I tried to do everything myself and once again found myself working twelve-hour workdays.

What happened to the freedom, flexibility, and control I promised myself?

In 2005, I gave birth to my son. He was born five weeks early when my doctor induced labor after diagnosing me with HELLP Syndrome, a form of severe preeclampsia. My liver was failing, and my platelet count was extremely low, so I had to give birth immediately. Before my diagnosis, I fully intended to work until my son's due date, so I was in the middle of several projects that ground to a sudden halt while I recovered in the hospital. I didn't even have time to let my clients know I had to stop working to give birth.

Because I spent so much of my career putting my work first, even while recovering from what could've been a fatal condition, I worried incessantly about the projects I put on hold. Sure, I spent time with my infant son, but I also found a way to sneak onto one of the hospital computers to email my clients and tell them why I suddenly disappeared.

I found dozens of emails from my clients, "Where are you? We need this done immediately! Why won't you answer me? What happened? Why isn't this already done?"

I convinced my husband to bring my laptop to the hospital so I could work when my son slept. And because I wasn't resting when I was supposed to be recovering from a traumatic birth, I spent more than a week in the hospital.

I remember asking my husband, "What's wrong with me?"

My husband was a firefighter, and he worked 24-hour shifts followed by 72 hours of time off, so we took turns watching our son while the other worked. We both still needed to sleep and spend time with our son, so that gave me about 30 hours per week to do everything I previously did in about twice the time. While I was making enough money to cover my bills, with fewer hours available to work, it wasn't the great money I previously earned.

After about two years of juggling work and family, I felt utterly exhausted, overwhelmed, and hopeless. It didn't help that my marriage was also a hot mess on the brink of complete collapse, the story of which I could fill an entire book. I found myself contemplating suicide to escape my situation. The horror of what that would do to my son was a wake-up call, and I sought help.

After some trial and error, my psychiatrist found a medication that worked for me, but I was still overwhelmed and exhausted. My therapist told me, "Something has to change."

Standing once again on the precipice of burnout, a bleak realization pushed me to reassess my approach and seek ways to break the insidious cycle. I had to accept that I couldn't do it all alone. I needed to build a team to alleviate the workload. I wasn't sure how I could hire someone when I wasn't earning as much as I had before my son was born. *How would I pay them?*

I took the leap anyway and hired my first employee after incorporating my business as an LLC in 2008. She was a good friend who wanted to earn extra money, and I brought her in as my office manager. At first, I found it challenging to delegate tasks because I was afraid she wouldn't do things my way, which I knew deep within my soul was the right way. I'm a perfectionist to my core! I still wanted to try to do everything, but I realized I had to let go of something.

She told me, "I can do it. Trust me!"

So, I did. She took over my bookkeeping and several other tasks, and I found that my worries were all for naught. She did a great job, and while those tasks usually required only a few hours of work each week, taking them off my plate provided immediate relief. Plus, I was able to use those hours to do more client work, so I was quickly able to cover her salary.

What else can I take off my plate?

Over the next few months, I outsourced my accounting to a CPA and found a freelance designer to collaborate with. I also hired two part-time junior developers to offload some of the client work so I could focus more on tasks I excelled at and enjoyed. Those first two developers didn't have much experience, but I trained them to do simple tasks I didn't want to do myself, and they did a great job. As I delegated tasks, I found myself with more time. That flexibility I yearned for when I started my freelance business was within reach.

As my business grew, I hired more developers, another project manager, and a salesperson. However, I made the mistake of hiring a few of those people based on my still-limited budget instead of their skills. I thought they were "good enough," and like my junior developers, I thought they would quickly learn. I was wrong. The salesperson I hired made grandiose promises to potential clients that my inexperienced team simply could not deliver. That left me with some angry clients.

One client told me, "You need to make this right!"

To meet their expectations, I had to pay another set of developers to do the project correctly. My attempt to save money by hiring a team with less experience and lower rates cost me significantly more than if I had just hired experts in the first place. It also cost me the goodwill of the clients that the inexperienced team worked with.

Quality work pays for itself. The time and effort saved by having experts on board are invaluable.

I let the inexperienced team go and found some experienced developers to help with larger projects I couldn't handle independently. Those developers cost considerably more than my previous team, but they had significantly more experience. They produced high-quality work, and I finally understood that the efficiency and proficiency of seasoned professionals would far outweigh any upfront cost differences. By entrusting critical tasks to the best in the industry, I was not only saving time and resources but also ensuring that the resulting work exceeded expectations.

And indeed, my decision to invest in top-tier talent proved to be a game-changer. Projects were completed faster, with fewer errors, and the results were consistently exceptional. Not only did this elevate the reputation of my business, but it also translated into increased client satisfaction, more repeat business, and many referrals.

A longtime client confided that she thought about hiring someone else for our ongoing work because of my inexperienced team, but she said, "I'm glad I stuck with you because now your work is even better than it was before."

I also experienced the flip side of the situation. On several occasions, potential clients came to me with a project, but after going with a less-experienced company because they were also less expensive, they returned to me to do the job the right way. They spent considerably more in the long run because they paid the first company for their shoddy work but also had to pay me what I originally quoted.

As I reflect on my journey, I'm grateful for the decision to seek out and invest in the best talent available, not only within web development but in all aspects of my business. Not only did it lead to tangible business growth, but it also enriched our collective experience and reaffirmed the importance of collaboration, innovation, and constant improvement. I do still sometimes hire less-experienced team members, including interns, but I provide them with training and give them tasks appropriate for their skill levels.

Ultimately, the courage to embrace top-tier talent, invest in their capabilities, and nurture a culture of excellence became the driving force behind my business's sustained success. As you embark on your own path, remember that seeking out the best of the best is not a luxury but a necessity. This investment will undoubtedly yield invaluable returns and set the stage for a future that knows no bounds.

THE PRACTICE

Delegating can be difficult, but keeping yourself out of the burnout cycle is necessary to allow your business to grow. I follow a four-step process whenever I start to feel overwhelmed by my responsibilities. This process isn't revolutionary, but I think it's important to share so you know you aren't the only one who might be holding on to tasks that you should probably delegate.

Step 1: Evaluate Your Tasks

Make a list of all the tasks you handle in your business. Include everything, from the core tasks related to your expertise to administrative tasks like bookkeeping and answering emails. Then, divide the tasks into four categories:

1. Tasks that only you can do: These might be the tasks that require your specific expertise, your vision, or your decision-making skills.
2. Tasks you enjoy but need training to accomplish efficiently: These are tasks that someone else can do, but you would eventually like to do yourself.
3. Tasks that you can do, but others could too (and probably should): This could include administrative tasks, client management, or any other tasks that are necessary but don't require your unique skills or might be done better by someone else.
4. Tasks that you shouldn't be doing: These are tasks that drain your time and energy. They might also include tasks you don't do efficiently and don't have the time or desire to learn.

Don't fall into the trap of putting everything into the first two categories. I'm a perfectionist, and I thought everything was in those categories for far too long. As much as you might want to do it all, you really can't do that and avoid burnout. Plus, if you aren't an expert on a particular task, it might be a much better use of your time and money to delegate than trying to do it yourself.

Step 2: Decide What to Delegate

After you categorize your tasks, start with the ones in the fourth category—those you shouldn't be doing. Make a list of those tasks and start thinking about who can handle them. They might be mundane administrative or highly specialized tasks that fall outside your expertise. Remember, the goal is to free up your time so you can focus on tasks that directly contribute to your business growth, that you excel at, and that you enjoy.

For the third category—tasks that you can do, but others can too—think about the cost-effectiveness and feasibility of delegating these tasks. If it would be cheaper or more efficient for someone else to handle these tasks, add them to your delegation list.

For tasks in the second category, consider what is required to gain the skills so you can do them yourself. If you have the desire, time, and money to learn how to do them, plan to do that. However, if you find that you don't have the time or money, add those tasks to your delegation list until you can do the training.

The tasks in the first category should stay on your to-do list.

Step 3: Find People to Delegate to

Now that you have a list of tasks to delegate, it's time to find the right people.

For delegating tasks within your existing team, look for people whose skills and interests align with the tasks and who can take on more work. You don't want your team to burn out! If you have a team member who doesn't have the necessary skills but wants to do the task and can acquire the skills with some training, consider whether getting that training is a viable option. And remember that adding skills to your team's repertoire can lead to more opportunities for your business in the future.

If you're outsourcing or need to hire someone to do a task, start by asking your network for recommendations. Someone you know might already know someone who can do what you need. You could also consider agencies that provide services like virtual assistance, bookkeeping, or web development. And if you *are* looking for a web developer, I have you covered.

Before deciding on a service provider or employee, interview potential candidates or service providers to assess their skills and fit for your company culture. Remember that while it's tempting to go with the least expensive option, that might cost you more in the long run. Try to find the most skilled candidate or service provider you can afford. If a task is mission-critical but doesn't need to be done immediately, you might even consider saving up to hire someone to do it right the first time.

Step 4: Delegate or Outsource Effectively

Once you've found the right people, it's time to delegate. Clearly communicate the tasks, expectations, metrics for success, and deadlines. Provide any necessary training and resources to ensure they can perform the tasks efficiently.

Regular check-ins and feedback sessions ensure everyone completes tasks as expected and promptly addresses any issues. However, avoid micromanaging—it not only defeats the purpose of delegation but can also lower morale and productivity.

Remember, delegation is a process. You might encounter obstacles and need to adjust. Be patient and open to feedback, and remember that the ultimate goal is to free up your time so you can focus on driving your business forward.

Chrissy Rey didn't start as a web developer but as a zoologist. While in college in the early nineties, she spent a summer volunteering at the local zoo, where she had the chance to work with orangutans, gorillas, monkeys, and many other animals. Shortly after college, through a series of twists and turns, she became a web developer and eventually became an expert in Flash. After hitting a few glass ceilings and burning out a couple of times, Chrissy decided she needed to start a company that did things differently, and that's how Pongos Interactive was born. Driven by a deep sense of community, Pongos Interactive aims to revolutionize the web development industry by offering WordPress solutions tailored to small businesses and nonprofits while promoting a culture that values work-life balance and amplifies underrepresented voices. If you need to delegate your online presence, Chrissy and her team of experts at Pongos Interactive can help with done-for-you packages. Visit pongos.com to get started. Chrissy also created the Website Success Academy to help solopreneurs who aren't quite ready to outsource everything but need expert help to do things the right way (if that's something in category two for you). You can find that at https://websitesuccessacademy.com/

Chapter 8

CANNABIS SOLUTIONS

Creating Curiosity in a Growing Wellness Field

Michelle Briggs, Psychiatric Mental Health Nurse Practitioner and Cannabis Nurse

"The evidence is overwhelming that marijuana can relieve certain types of pain, nausea, vomiting, and other symptoms caused by such illnesses as multiple sclerosis, cancer, and AIDS— or by the harsh drugs sometimes used to treat them. And it can do so with remarkable safety. Indeed, marijuana is less toxic than many of the drugs that physicians prescribe every day."- Joycelyn Elders, Former Surgeon General of the United States.

"The cannabis plant has more potential than any other plant on earth."- Dr. Sanjay Gupta, an American neurosurgeon and medical correspondent.

"Make the most of the hemp seed, sow it everywhere."- George Washington, First President of the United States.

MY STORY

"Hello, Code Green Healthcare. May I help you?" I said, listening for the voice of a patient to respond.

"Hi, uh, I was wondering…ah, I'm looking for a way to use marijuana, and the people at the dispensary told me you could help me out. I can't use opioids; that shit almost killed me."

"Of course. Why don't you tell me about yourself and your medical conditions."

He told me his story: "I was in a car accident a while back, and now I can't sleep; my back is killing me. And I work a construction job. I got onto pills, but the doctor just cut them off one day, so I found myself looking for pills on the street."

He paused. "I just got detoxed. Do you know how hard it is to find a place to detox you? I tried to stop cold turkey, but I got so sick that I just couldn't. I was puking, shaking, and had the chills. Ma'am, I almost lost everything—my wife, kids, my job. I think that marijuana can help, and I want to go legal. I hurt so bad every day. But I can't do those goddamn pills!" He was angry.

Who knew that my journey in nursing would lead me to a wellness career in cannabis? But giving people who've known suffering, struggle, and loss access to healing has always been the goal. The benefits of cannabis are one more route. A natural one.

I've been attracted to natural options for healing since I was a young child. I created potions with shampoo, leaves, and spices and gave the liquid to my sick doll. I rubbed a plant leaf and mud on my friend's knee when she fell on the concrete playing hopscotch. I was fascinated by science and medicine. Since the age of fifteen, I've been working in healthcare. Helping people has always been my passion. My career purpose is healing physical, emotional, or spiritual pain. I've traveled from wearing plastic nurse gear from the five and dime to a master's degree in psychiatric and mental health nursing—a career path that led me to multiple leadership roles and now finds me a holistic cannabis nurse entrepreneur.

Entering the cannabis medicine field took courage. I still get perplexed and disapproving looks from friends, family, and colleagues when I announce that I own a California cannabis farm and a company that helps patients access medical marijuana. People continue to have fears and biases toward marijuana despite legalization and evidenced-based research supporting its safe use. Overcoming stigma in any profession can be challenging, but with persistence and education, it's possible.

Starting a career in this controversial field prompted me to address my own relationship with cannabis. If you go out on a limb and build a business in the taboo cannabis industry, you better understand your own history with it.

I started "self-medicating" with marijuana illegally in the eighties. I was in high school, and in retrospect, I used it as medication. At the time, like many young girls, I was fighting the waves of hormonal fluctuations. I also had undiagnosed post-traumatic stress syndrome from adoptee trauma. Marijuana, when I could get it, helped my PMS and the fears that haunted my mind. Although I used it, I worried I'd be arrested. Or, I'd smoke a joint and go wild like in the movie *Reefer Madness*.

Or worse yet, marijuana would be the gateway to using cocaine or heroin. People die when they use those drugs. None of these things happened to me, yet I feared they would.

When I entered nursing school, I no longer used marijuana for fear of getting caught and losing my career opportunity. A few months after stopping it, I experienced suicidal depression and feared losing my mind and failing out of school. I sought help from the campus psychiatrist. When I told her I found relief from my symptoms when I used marijuana in the past, she told me I should consider getting drug treatment and sent me to a group with other students with alcohol and drug "problems." I felt shame that I used marijuana and never used it again until years later. She also prescribed me psychotropics with uncomfortable side effects. Oh, how I wish I was offered a natural option of cannabis at the time. Rather than muting my moods and trauma symptoms with psychiatric drugs, I could've learned how to medicate with natural cannabis and allowed myself a more empathic and holistic healing journey.

Cannabis wasn't legal until California passed the Compassion Use Act in 1996. Slowly more states became legal as acceptance was driven by growing scientific evidence and anecdotal reports suggesting its potential therapeutic benefits. Today, cannabis "medication"—which dates back thousands of years and was used in ancient civilizations such as China, Egypt, and India—is medically legal in 40 states, including the District of Columbia. The recreational or adult use of cannabis has been approved in 23 states and the District of Columbia. My own state established the Maryland Medical Cannabis Program in 2014. The program allows patients with qualifying medical conditions to obtain a medical marijuana card and purchase cannabis products from licensed dispensaries.

The legalization in Maryland ignited my entrepreneurial spirit. I already owned a farm, so why not offer this medication to residents of Maryland? Helping patients improve their quality of life with cannabis was an obvious extension of my life's work—and I had a genuine passion for cannabis and its potential benefits. I could see that starting a cannabis business was a way to contribute to the industry and advocate for its responsible use. I wanted to innovate and educate—and I was willing to take risks. I could create job opportunities and enter a potentially lucrative emerging market. The medical cannabis industry has shown significant potential for generating profits. With the demand increasing and legal restrictions easing in many places, a medical cannabis business could be profitable if I could navigate the legal and regulatory complexities.

Quickly I was on the road to starting Code Green Healthcare, LLC (CGH) and learning what I needed to know to become a successful cannabis nurse entrepreneur. The American Cannabis Nurses Association (ACNA) had educational resources and provided me with certification. The ACNA mission: "To advance excellence in cannabis nursing practice through advocacy, collaboration, education, research, and policy development," also became my mission.

I also became familiar with a quickly growing coalition of other national medical cannabis advocacy groups such as Americans for Safe Access (ASA), The Cannabis Consumers Coalition (CCC), Marijuana Policy Project (MPP), Drug Policy Alliance (DPA), National Organization for Reform of Marijuana Laws (NORML), Veterans Cannabis Coalition (VCC), The Weed for Warriors Project (W4WP) and Minorities for Medical Marijuana (M4MM).

I continue to be curious about cannabis and advocate for its use where medically appropriate. This curiosity has driven me to explore, discover, and learn more about the medicinal qualities of the cannabis plant. I have gained a deeper understanding of the potential for cannabis to heal patients physically, emotionally, and spiritually.

Today I spoke with a parent of a nine-year-old daughter diagnosed with autism. She was distraught and frustrated that "the medications her doctor gives her don't make her feel better." She told me how the psychiatrist prescribed five psychiatric medications for her daughter, and she feared the side effects were "hurting her more than helping her." I explained that the use of cannabis, specifically CBD oil, for children with autism is still a topic of ongoing research and debate. However, some parents may choose this route due to anecdotal evidence suggesting that it may help to manage specific symptoms associated with autism. I was happy to educate her on using medical marijuana for her daughter and encourage her to continue consultation with her other medical professional. I've recommended cannabis for other children over the years, and all of the parents have reported improvements in symptoms, including seizures, anxiety, irritability, and problems with sleep and focus.

Although there's limited evidenced-based research on the effectiveness of cannabis in treating various medical conditions, including autism, some studies have shown potential benefits of cannabis in specific areas such as epilepsy, chronic pain, nausea and vomiting, multiple sclerosis, anorexia, generalized anxiety, depression, insomnia, Parkinson's disease and more. It's important to note that the research on cannabis is still evolving, and more rigorous studies are needed to fully understand its potential benefits and risks.

Medical marijuana might not be for you. It's okay. Let's face it, like any medication, medical cannabis can have side effects, primarily when individuals use high doses. Medical cannabis could have drug interactions. It's essential to consult with a healthcare professional before using it, especially if you are taking other medications. You may be worried about dependency and addiction. While medical cannabis is considered to have a lower risk of addiction than other substances, it's still possible to develop a dependence on it. Cannabis can also impair judgment and cognition, leading to an increased risk of accidents and injuries, especially when driving or operating machinery. It's important for individuals considering medical cannabis to thoroughly educate themselves about its potential benefits and dangers and consult with a healthcare professional who is knowledgeable in this area.

I also encourage you to explore your biases and the stigma surrounding this ancient medication before you make any judgments. Understanding and challenging our biases can help ensure we make decisions based on evidence and compassion rather than preconceived notions or stigmatization.

THE PRACTICE

Cannabis as a Business

Starting a business in the United States that promotes a product or service that is stigmatized and federally illegal can be very scary. I have overcome my fears and helped others choose personal freedom to use cannabis without fear of legal repercussions in my state.

Maybe you want to start a marijuana business or a business that could be controversial, taboo, or stigmatized. Before starting this business, here are some ways to reduce your biases, fears, and stigma.

1. Education: Learn as much as possible about your industry, including legal and societal views. Understanding the realities of the industry can help dispel myths and misinformation.
2. Get to know the market: Understand who your customers will be and what they want. This can help reduce fear of the unknown and help you make informed and well-supported decisions about your business.
3. Connect with industry professionals: Seek mentors or advisors already in your industry. They can provide valuable insights and information, and their support can help reduce fears and stigma.
4. Develop a strong business plan: A well-thought-out business plan will guide your decision-making and give you confidence in your venture. This can help alleviate fears and doubts.
5. Recognize any biases you may have and challenge them. This could involve seeking diverse perspectives,

questioning your assumptions and where they originate from, and being open to new information.

6. Use professional language: Using scientific and business terms instead of slang can help to legitimize your business and reduce stigma.

7. Focus on the benefits: Whether it's a healing property, economic benefit, or the potential for social justice, focusing on the positive aspects of your industry can help shift your perspective and remove barriers.

8. Practice transparency: Be open and honest about your business practices. This can help build trust and credibility.

9. Seek legal advice: Understanding the legal landscape of your industry can help reduce fears and uncertainty. Consult with a lawyer or legal expert to ensure you comply with all regulations.

Remember, it's natural to have concerns when starting a new business, especially in a controversial industry.

Cannabis for your Personal and Professional Health

Maybe you're a business leader like me and want to use the medical marijuana program in your state. Here's how you could benefit from its use.

1. Stress and Anxiety Reduction: Running a business can be stressful. Medical marijuana can help reduce anxiety and promote a sense of calm, allowing business owners to better cope with the demands of their professional lives.

2. Pain Relief: If a business leader suffers from a condition that causes chronic pain, medical marijuana could help manage this pain, potentially leading to increased focus and productivity.

3. Improved Sleep: Sleep disorders can affect a person's ability to function effectively during the day. Medical marijuana may help enhance sleep quality, leading to better decision-making and cognitive function.

4. Enhanced productivity and motivation: Some individuals find that marijuana can increase their motivation and productivity levels. This can be especially helpful for those individuals who struggle with depression, anxiety, or lack of enthusiasm in their professional lives.

5. Symptom relief for menstrual-related issues for women: Medical marijuana can alleviate symptoms associated with menstruation, such as cramps, bloating, and mood swings. Women can maintain focus and productivity throughout their menstrual cycle by reducing these symptoms.

It's important to note that the benefits of medical marijuana can vary depending on the individual and their specific needs. Consulting with a healthcare professional or a medical marijuana specialist is recommended to determine the most suitable treatment options.

Michelle Briggs, Psychiatric Mental Health Nurse Practitioner, is the CEO of Code Green Healthcare, LLC, specializing in using cannabinoid therapeutics in Maryland. She has a Bachelor's of Nursing from Johns Hopkins University School of Nursing and a Master's of Nursing from the University of Maryland School of Nursing.

She spent 30 years in psychiatric nursing practice, and 6 of those have included recommending cannabis and other holistic healing modalities. She is a psychotherapist, educator, co-host for women's retreats, and entrepreneur in the cannabis industry.

Michelle believes in the physical, mental, and spiritual healing gifts of cannabis medicine. She is currently enrolled in a certification program for psychedelic-assisted psychotherapy with the hope of offering this treatment modality to patients in the near future.

When she's not building her business and serving her patients, Michelle spends time with her twin teenage sons and niece or dog, Jake. She also is a member of the 12-Step AlaNon group. Michelle also finds joy and stress relief in riding her jetski on the Chesapeake Bay and music. Thanks to support from her husband, John, she can explore her entrepreneurial dreams.

Connect with Michelle:

Website: https://www.codegreenhealthcare.com/
Facebook: https://www.facebook.com/Codegreenhealthcare
Instagram: https://www.instagram.com/code_green_healthcare
LinkedIn: https://www.linkedin.com/in/michelle-briggs-a34a6875/
Email: michellebriggs@codegreenhealth.com

Chapter 9

STEP INTO YOUR STORY

The Secret to Confident Brand Visibility that Drives Sales

Maureen Porto, Brand Marketing Strategist and Commercial Photographer

MY STORY

"Maureen, these photos look great. It's. . .uh. . .it's just that it's starting to bother me that you're not in them. Not even one. I know I've said this to you before, but I really think you should pick up that tripod and figure out how to shoot on a timer so you can get in some of these photos instead of always capturing everyone else."

Ugh. *This* conversation. *Again.*

I twisted the cap off the white bottle, pulled open the drawer, and fished around for the letter opener. There were plastic kid's scissors, a couple of ballpoint pens without caps, and two dull dinner knives that easily would've done the trick, but I still wanted the letter opener. Ever since I could remember, it sat on my grandfather's mahogany drop-lid desk in his Brooklyn brownstone, and something about the shape and weight of the tarnished silver always felt comforting in my palm. I stabbed the top of the developer, tugged on the tab, and slowly poured the chemical into the warm water waiting in the tray.

The darkroom was always my escape. The dim red lights were like a comforting blanket from the rest of the world.

Why are we talking about this again? Why here? I should make a sign for the basement door: no light or uncomfortable conversations allowed in this sacred space.

I was weeks away from my 12th birthday that summer in 1986, and the first wispy clouds of self-consciousness had started to blow my way. Even decades before the birth of social media, Photoshop, and the rise of impossible beauty standards, I had already begun to notice my shortcomings. In just the last few weeks, I realized that my two front teeth dominate my mouth at twice the size of the others, a friend commented on the freckles that litter my nose, and yesterday, I discovered that my right eye doesn't open nearly as wide as my left eye.

Let's be honest. I wasn't about to document any of this on Kodachrome film.

How do I explain this to my Dad, the man responsible for half of my DNA? How do I tell him that I don't like my looks? How could I ever feel comfortable in photos when I had no idea how to pose or smile, and I just felt stupid in every shot?

I spent countless hours pouring over my mother's Good Housekeeping magazines. As soon as the new issue arrived, I would slip the old one onto the stack in my bedroom and fall asleep studying the flawless faces of Jaclyn Smith, Connie Selleca, and Debby Boone. I drank in every detail of their makeup, clothing, and the casual ways they angled their faces and bodies. It was all so simple and easy for these natural beauties who commanded attention with their laid-back elegance in every frame.

How does she smile without flashing her pink gums? How does she have so much expression in her eyes without scrunching up her whole face? Why doesn't she look angry like I do when she's not smiling?

I decided then that staying on the sidelines was the safest place for me, and I spent the next decade or so doing my best to avoid photos and their feelings of awkwardness and discomfort. It doesn't take an expert like Carl Jung to recognize that the countless hours I spent developing my photography skills were likely some unconscious attempt to secure my place safely behind the camera so I wouldn't have to appear in front of it!

Let's face it, as human beings, we're wired to notice what's wrong or what isn't working more than what is right. It's a deep-rooted survival mechanism meant to keep us safe from dangerous situations.

The inner critic we all have within us is different from this. It whispers to us with harsh judgment and controlling thoughts as a dysfunctional way of coping with guilt, fear, uncomfortable feelings, and even the unknown. It's easy to let that voice control you, but negative self-talk is toxic. It causes anxiety, shame, and deep insecurities. In order to deal with that anxiety and shame, the inner critic then triggers procrastination and avoidance in order to reduce those feelings and stay "safe" while playing small.

I've done the work to learn specific exercises to recognize my inner critic and the harmful ways I've spoken to myself, and I've worked hard to shed my insecurities and rewrite the old narratives rattling around my brain so I can feel comfortable putting myself out there again. I now know that I'm in control of how I think. I can process events and experiences in a way that'll either push me forward or hold me back; the choice is mine alone.

As a brand marketing strategist, I've learned the undeniable correlation between visibility and success, and I've made it my life's work to support other businesswomen who struggle as I did. It's fueled my passion to help ambitious, camera-shy professionals create beautiful, eye-catching business photos that attract ideal attention, jumpstart authentic connections, and drive sales.

The simple truth is, people won't know you exist unless you put yourself out there!

Big companies hire marketing teams tasked with building awareness, increasing reach, and driving conversions, but your true goal as a marketer is simple: to get the customer to know, like, and trust your brand (which organically leads them to purchase the product and service). The best way to build that know, like, and trust factor is to show up authentically and allow people to see the real you.

You can have the best product or services in the world, but if no one knows about it, they won't buy it. Most people assume that businesses with the highest quality service or products are the ones who automatically get the most customers. In fact, the scientific reality is that every business must pass a popularity contest before an ability contest. Consumers consider visibility equal to credibility. This is why influencers in your feed have more power to persuade you than a random commercial or ad in a magazine. If consumers don't know who you are, they won't choose you, so investing in your business's visibility is an investment in its sustainability and success. Your ideal clients, the ones you genuinely want to serve, are waiting for you to show up if you're brave enough to do so.

For this reason, it's not possible to overstate the power of visibility. When a business has a visible presence, it captures the audience's attention and encourages action. Consistent visibility helps increase exposure to larger audiences, and when people know who you are and how you can solve their problems, you begin to build brand recognition. Brand recognition helps establish trust, which is essential when creating a solid customer base. When clients trust a brand, they become loyal customers and repeat buyers and are much more likely to recommend your brand to others.

The good news is that the opportunity to grow your business and crush your goals has never been stronger than it is *right now*. Consumers are in a feeding frenzy of user-generated content like never before in the history of mankind. With TikTok, Instagram,

Meta, YouTube, Pinterest, Twitter, Linkedin, and countless podcasts, we live at a moment in time when your brand can reach almost anyone on Earth if you're willing to put yourself out there.

That's thrilling news, but understandably, the pressure to be visible can also feel overwhelming for most people.

Maybe you're new to entrepreneurship. Change can be hard, and what's new is often uncomfortable for most people. If you're not used to being the face and voice of your business or selling and marketing yourself, this can initially feel awkward.

Maybe you're one of the five million new businesses formed last year or stepping into a new identity within your company. It's natural and typical for this new role to bring up some feelings of impostor syndrome.

Maybe you're an introvert or a highly sensitive person. If you're an introvert, you may not feel natural and comfortable in front of the camera or the microphone. If you're a highly sensitive person, your nervous system can easily be overwhelmed with all the stimuli present when it comes to being visible online.

Other people don't realize they carry past trauma wounds around being seen and heard. It's common for intelligent, powerful women to struggle with feelings of unworthiness and doubt. For generations, the narrative has been that good girls are muted and well-behaved and should stay seated quietly in the classroom or at home, so it's no wonder many women are now uncomfortable when it's time to stand up, speak out, or take the lead.

You can't escape the effects of unresolved trauma or past experiences; even in business, these fears often pop up and appear as blocks right as you step into the spotlight.

The good news is that with some work, you, too, can heal and release these mindset blocks, making it easy to show up authentically and confidently in your business.

Visibility mindset blocks are much more common than people realize. Being visible means being vulnerable. As a business owner, visibility is mandatory for success because *you* are the one that clients choose to work with and trust. To attract clients, you must establish trust and credibility, and you can only do that by being authentic and visible.

Being visible brings up fears of being seen. Many of us struggle with being seen (*where are my introverted entrepreneurs?*). The thing to remember is that the fear of being seen is more common than you may realize. Allowing ourselves to be seen, whether on social media, a podcast, or even a discovery call, can bring all of these fears back to the surface.

With increased visibility comes other people's assumptions and opinions. Many clients I work with express concern about being judged or even ridiculed. This fear is real and can be debilitating if left unchecked. It can push talented professionals into playing small, and it's critically important to remember that these feelings can be overcome with a little work and practice.

I know it can feel challenging at times. I understand all of the self-doubt, insecurities, and not enough-ness that comes up when you decide you want more because I have walked that path (and I continue to!), and I have the tools available to help you.

Let's do this!

> *"Our deepest fear is not that we are inadequate. Our deepest fear is that we are powerful beyond measure. It is our light, not our darkness, that most frightens us. We ask ourselves, 'Who am I to be brilliant, gorgeous, talented, fabulous?' Actually, who are you not to be? You are a child of God. Your playing small does not serve the world. There is nothing enlightened about shrinking so that other people won't feel insecure around you. We are all meant to shine, as children do. We were born to make manifest the glory of God that is within us. It's not just in some of us; it's in everyone. And as we let our own light shine, we unconsciously give other people permission to do the same. As we are liberated from our own fear, our presence automatically liberates others."*
> ~Marianne Williamson

THE PRACTICE

Now that we know the importance of visibility, it's important to recognize that getting visible often requires doing deeper work.

So often when people are struggling with visibility, they want to know what to say to their audience and how to say it. While your messaging is an important part of connecting with your audience, it's not the first, or even the most important, part.

The first and most important part is addressing your thoughts, feelings, and experiences around being visible in the first place.

It's here that we'll address and release those parts of us that whisper that we're not good enough, the part that continues to live in lack, the part that craves the comfort of playing safe and small.

For many of us, that means recognizing and healing unidentified trauma wounds around being seen and heard as a child. Before you skip ahead, remember that trauma is an inevitable part of the human journey, and it doesn't have to be dramatic or abusive in order to exist. Even harmless comments, criticisms, and encounters from years ago can leave unrealized damage that continues to affect our unconscious thoughts, habits, behaviors, and beliefs.

These wounds are unavoidable and completely personal to each of us, so let go of any judgment, embarrassment, or shame you may feel when exploring your shadows. Instead, give yourself grace, plenty of time to rest, and even some applause for bravely doing the difficult but rewarding work of healing.

Fortunately for us, our wounds can be uncovered and healed through inner work, including:

- Mindset work of examining your thoughts and beliefs around being seen and showing up in your business.

- Somatic work of tapping into your feelings and bodily sensations that come up when it's time to be visible.

When you're willing to do the deeper shadow work, you can unlock the limitless power of knowing and guiding yourself, and you'll begin to show up more authentically and confidently in your business and in your life.

When you're ready to begin, you may consider finding some uninterrupted time to journal honestly and without reservation about the following:

- How did you experience being seen and heard as a child?
- Were you ever shut down, ignored, or told to be quiet?
- How did people react when you were "the real you"?
- What parts of you did you learn to hide in order to feel accepted?

Each of us develops different coping mechanisms based on our own personalities and experiences. Often in the examples above, we did what we felt was required to manage the situation or meet others' expectations. Many times that means shutting down when we want to speak up or behaving in certain ways to please other people, and not necessarily in ways that reflect our authentic self.

When we don't do the inner work to address these experiences, we grow into adults who continue to hold back from being visible and prevent ourselves from showing up with authenticity and confidence in our lives and businesses.

Even if we *want* to be our authentic selves, to share our work, to speak up, we may still feel some resistance when actually doing it. That rub is the indicator that something is present in the deeper shadows of ourselves that needs to be unpacked and healed. Keep going, Sister!

Shifting our mindset is a big part of this journey. The most successful people in history credit the mindset as the single greatest asset that an entrepreneur has. Think about that for a moment. It's ours, it's free, and it's available to each of us.

Mindset is determined by each of us alone and something we have to work on daily. It's critical that we make mindset work a consistent part of our routine because there is so much negative news and draining stimuli in the world these days, and we have to prioritize a healthy mindset and mental state.

As business owners, we hire tax accountants, graphic designers, business coaches, and other experts who help maximize our business revenue. By the same token, we need to evaluate what we're doing to work on our mental health. How are we showing up for ourselves and our mindset?

Being an entrepreneur means navigating new obstacles daily. Having the right mindset is critical to success. It begins with remembering that we're in control of how we think. We can choose to process experiences in a way that will either push us forward or hold us back, and the choice is ours alone.

Let's get to the fun part! This is the exact 3-step formula I've used myself countless times and with clients to identify and heal mindset blocks:

Step 1: Uncover Your Fears

In order to rewrite your fears (or limiting beliefs/stories), you need to be honest with yourself about what you're really afraid of.

If you're scared of being judged, ask yourself WHY you're scared of being judged. How does being judged make you feel? Allow yourself to imagine every detail of this judgment and sit with these feelings, no matter how uncomfortable they make you. Breathe and begin to dive into the root cause of your fear and your feelings surrounding it, not just the surface fear.

Whose face is it you see when you feel judged? Is it someone from your past, your present, strangers online, or your own inner critic? If it's someone else's face you see, remember that people will always have an opinion and begin the practice of resisting letting other people define you and your value.

If it's your own inner critic you fear, do a quick and compassionate self-audit. Acknowledge what you are good at, and don't be afraid to own up to things you're not. Let go of any urge to be perfect. If there are tangible changes you want to make to feel more confident - start to invest in yourself! Hire a trainer or just start walking, budget for a stylist to pick pieces that compliment your figure and style, get a facial, take the art class, book that vacation, pull out the good china, talk to yourself like you would a good girlfriend, and begin today to make yourself a priority.

Step 2: Flip the Script!

Now that you know what you're afraid of, it's time to transform those limiting beliefs (fears) into a new set of *empowering* beliefs.

Remember that a belief is just something you repeat to yourself over and over. If you repeatedly tell yourself you can't go live on Facebook because you'll forget your thoughts, then that's exactly what will happen.

But if you repeatedly tell yourself you love live video and can't wait to share your message with your audience, guess what? You'll begin to LOVE live video.

Step 3: Reprogram Your Mind

Girlfriend, here is the dirty little secret no one tells you: *You get to decide what you believe about yourself.*

Once you have created your new list of empowering beliefs, create a sentence or two that embodies these new beliefs. This sentence becomes an affirmation that you repeat to yourself **EVERY. SINGLE. DAY.**

Repeating this positive affirmation will reprogram your subconscious mind, and this affirmation will become your new story and, soon enough - your new reality.

Remember, this takes some consistent practice and might feel prickly and maybe even a little fake when you begin. That's okay, don't stop. Remember that you are not alone in these feelings, and push through them. As Steven Pressfield, author of *The War of Art,* says, "The more important something is to our soul's evolution, the more resistance we will feel toward pursuing it.". *Keep going, Sister!*

I can tell you from experience that the deepest resistance came up when I began sharing my soul gifts.

But that's also when I experienced the greatest rewards - when I finally conquered my own fear of being visible.

That, my friend, is why it's so critically important to do the work of healing, realizing that we are here on purpose and for a purpose. When we recognize that our true power lies not in being *more* or being someone else but in radically accepting and revealing who we have been created to be, we are not only free to share our soul gifts, but we allow countless others to benefit from them as well.

Maureen Porto is an award-winning portrait photographer passionate about helping ambitious, camera-shy professionals create beautiful, eye-catching headshots and elevated marketing images that are known to attract ideal audience attention and drive results.

Having spent far too long feeling awkward and uncomfortable in front of the camera, Maureen made it her mission to increase the visibility of professional women by designing a relaxing and fully guided process that eliminates overwhelm and ensures her clients feel comfortable and confident every step of the way.

Over the last 15 years, her work has been featured in countless local and national publications, including Forbes, Washingtonian, People Magazine, Elle, and House Beautiful. The portraits she creates in her Annapolis, Maryland studio and on location have earned her opportunities to photograph clients from coast to coast, including a wide variety of creatives, executives, politicians, and celebrities, but her most inspiring work is helping business women regain their confidence in front of the camera and amplify their unique value in order to further their impact in our communities.

On the weekend, you'll find her racing to the woods in her Sprinter RV, eager to unplug while dispersed camping, fly fishing, trail riding, and hiking with her husband, Mark (and on occasion, their two busy children, Jack and Olivia).

Connect with her here:

Website: https://www.maureenporto.com/
Facebook: https://www.Facebook.com/MaureenPortoStudios
Instagram: https://www.instagram.com/maureen.porto.studios/
Linkedin: https://www.linkedin.com/in/maureen-porto/

Chapter 10

WHAT'S LOVE GOT TO DO WITH IT?

Harness Your Superpower to Lead a Business (or Team) People Trust

Julie Campbell, President/CEO of the Severn Leadership Group

MY STORY

In my life, I've had the privilege to be a member of multiple teams, some great, some awful. As an eternal optimist, I've taken my lessons learned from those terrible teams and then let go of the rest (blame, resentment, "ick"). My winning teams have been as simple as the high school relay team that went to the regional finals or as disaster-averting as the Presidential Communications Command travel team that revived a temporary air-ground network minutes before the president's helicopter landed in a remote field. What made those teams great was not a single accomplishment or person. Greatness was achieved because of the character of the team members, from leader to follower (senior to junior member), as they worked toward their common purpose together.

Whether you choose to be the boss or were selected to be in a leadership position, you're fulfilling one of the greatest stations and noblest professions in life. While all of us were created to be in relationship with others, leadership is a relationship of influence—influencing others not to submit to your personal will but to support a common purpose or mission. Leaders change the world.

At the Severn Leadership Group (SLG), we say: "Leadership begins with you but is not about you." (Sig Berg, Founder SLG). We focus on leadership of teams. Why teams? Because with teams, you get more things done. With teams, the impact is multiplied. Whether it's an organized team of employees in your business, a team you create with a client or customer, or a multi-functional team that comes together around a shared purpose, when you invest in your team, you invest in your business. When you pour into your team, great things happen.

If you've been part of a high-performing team, you may remember the sweet feeling of success after arduous toil or the cheers from the crowd at the medal ceremony. But longer lasting and legacy leaving are the memories of the relationships that run deep and make the extraordinary team possible.

It takes time and intention to build a team of excellence. The members must invest in each other and the team's higher purpose. Whether by position (president, business owner) or role (director of planning, spiritual director), the leader sets the tone in their behavior toward others. Authentic behavior builds the trust needed to perform as a unified team. Don't we all desire teams or partnerships that exude excellence?

A vision that we will be there for each other until the end.

As a woman and leader in the military, information technology sector, nonprofit sector, and at home, I can think of no better example of a team of excellence than our (not "my") team of women from the Academy of Holy Angels (AHA) High School Class of 1985.

Our team has lasted the test of time, forged with our plaid Catholic uniform skirts and leg warmers of the 80s and made stronger through our shared history of struggles and successes. Our purpose has been to support each other's work and life journeys, challenge each other to level up wherever we lead or follow, and become difference-makers in this world. When all others are gone (parents, siblings, spouses), the women left standing will support each other however they can.

As daughters, wives, mothers, leaders, and followers in various professions, there is one superpower this band of sisters all inherently and naturally share and practice. For some of us, it's rooted in our faith. For others, it was introduced and modeled by our parents, older siblings, amazing teachers, or coaches. It's a reflection of each woman's character as we sharpen each other through the behaviors we display together as a team:

- Everyone is engaged and collaborates
- We are willing and open to learning

- Each knows their strengths and weaknesses and the others' gifts and shortcomings
- We hold each other accountable
- Encouragement and inspiration abound
- We celebrate successes
- No one suffers alone
- Respect, empathy, and compassion are practiced always
- Committed, we have faith in each other; no one is left behind

What is this superpower we all have inside us? It's a timeless, tested, and transcendent virtue we were created with. It's natural and free for all of us to tap into. It's a requirement for our team and needs to be exercised by every leader and follower of your team, business, or organization.

It is love.

Agape love is a selfless love for others, a genuine concern for our fellow man (woman). It's not just a feeling; it's an action word, a verb. Think of a Marine Corps platoon leader who always eats last, runs in the back of her Marines, checks her Marines' feet after long days in the battlefield, and ultimately would die for her Marines. That's the love I'm talking about!

You may know agape love as the Golden Rule. It's as old as Confucianism: "Do not do to others what you do not want them to do to you." (5th century BC), Buddhism: "Whatever is disagreeable to yourself, do not do unto others." (6th century BC) and Christianity: "Love your neighbor as yourself." (1st century AD).

As women, it comes naturally. We've practiced it as a band of girlfriends, with our siblings, significant others or spouses, and our children. We often volunteer because of our love for our community, fellow (wo)man, and the world. It's a superpower because it's in **our nature to love; We are designed to love**. We're looked at as a **source of love**. And when we dare to practice agape love outside our familial bonds, it reveals our authentic self; **it builds trust**.

As one of our recent SLG Fellows shared: "Equating leadership to loving my team/followers/coworkers has allowed me to be more empathetic and also be more authentic in the workplace." (Claire Gilbert, SLG 2021 Alumna.)

Who doesn't want to feel your love? When you bring to bear agape love in your business, workplace, and wherever you serve, who doesn't want to be a part of your team? And when your client or customer, employee, or coworker feels like they're a beloved member of the team, the character of your work and the world around you will be transformed. You'll bring hope and flourishing into a world that badly needs that right now.

"But," more than one SLG Fellow has stated, "how can I love others in my professional workplace?" They have missed the point. They don't understand agape love. They haven't experienced the bonds and the progress of a team that loves each other and those they work with.

One of my mentors and a great leader I worked for in the aerospace industry loves our country. He instilled in all of us, from our administrative assistant to the engineers who designed brilliant technological solutions, that our real (unstated) mission was "caring for America's sons and daughters." This tough "Army grunt" (I say that lovingly) loved all of us no matter our role because of our commitment to serving those who serve our country. He practiced agape love holding us accountable. He knew his weaknesses and tapped into our strengths to succeed at our mission. He always treated us with respect, empathy, and compassion, encouraging us to lead lives of integrity and excellence every day. We were "One Team, One Fight." If he could do it, so could you.

Why did I lead with the example of my team of high school classmates? How does that help you and me in our work today? It's easy to practice love with this team of women who've shaped me through the history we're shaping together. We sharpen each other and sharpen those outside this small circle through our shared experiences, trials, and triumphs.

The Behaviors of Love

Let's take a closer look at some of the behaviors of agape love that we practice as a team. Perhaps you'll see yourself as one of these women and how each uniquely behaves (treats others) with love. I hope you recognize the value of adopting many of the behaviors below (especially if they're absent in your behaviors) and begin to practice them in your work and life.

All of us have been served our slices of "humble pie" over the years. It's difficult to admit your mistakes to others. It takes humility and courage to speak up when you're wrong or weak. Over time, this trusted circle of women has come to know our imperfections. But instead of belaboring or dwelling on what we cannot do, we draw on our unique gifts and strengths to get the job done with excellence.

- Laura (Allora) is our designated "Leader" and planner extraordinaire. She has the gift of hospitality and is generous with her time and resources. She knows all of us well and plans all our time together with careful consideration for what each individual might need to thrive.
- Michele is our chaplain and coach. She serves as our "spiritual leader" with her heartfelt prayers and as our life coach, always asking deep questions and listening to learn with an empathetic ear. She reminds us of our ultimate leader and leads by example with her gentle spirit, quiet calmness, and infectious laugh.
- Jane (Janey) is our navigator, North Star, and rock of support. She's practical, intelligent, grounding, and high in emotional intelligence. Jane leaves no one behind. She believes in us, reminds us of our purpose, and is the glue that holds us together as a team.
- Kathy (Kate) brings humor, fun, grit, and joy. She "goes with the flow" and reminds us not to take ourselves too seriously. She has a heart for competition and encourages us to be our best no matter what we do, holding us accountable and cheering us on.
- Cynthia (Cyntho) is open, honest, and brave. She shines in her struggles and rebounds strongly from adversity. Cynthia knows herself and when to say "no" even when it's not the popular option. She's a model for all of us when we face our own challenges.
- Mary Lou (Louie) is a grand teacher in the classroom and in the art of being authentic. She shows us how to be beautifully genuine no matter what. She makes you

feel comfortable and at ease when conflict happens—
and it always happens with a team! How else can a
team create something innovative and amazing without
conflict?

- Meghan (Meg or Hannis) is caring and affectionate but
  also raw, direct, and willing to share mistakes, teaching
  us to stay humble in our everyday missteps.

- And then there is me (Big Julie). In the team's words:
  "Julie is patient and kind and will share her challenges
  honestly and openly. She knows what it means to serve
  others; she has lived that life. Julie brings our team
  credibility."

No one of us can do this alone. The making of greatness
is collaborative. Cultivating a high-performance team with
members that trust each other no matter what requires the
virtue of love and a dose of faith.

As children of the 80s, the music of the band U2 has been
a backdrop to our lives. The lead singer Bono shared in his
autobiography, *Surrender*, "We all shared faith. Faith in each
other. Faith that our coming together as musicians might prove
more than the sum of our parts." (p.136). Have faith that you
can make your team great with the power of love.

I want to help you hone your superpower by starting with
the familiar and by reflecting on those teams, those friendships
where it is easiest for you to practice agape love. Let's create
those conditions in your life practice to lead a business that
people trust and experience wonder as you see the world around
you prosper.

THE PRACTICE

Backdrop

In 2015, when I joined the Severn Leadership Group (SLG) as a mentor, I was leading in the military and technical industries with "my style" which I equated to being like a "sister" to others. I operated with empathy and compassion and with doses of tough love and the desire to challenge others to be the best so as a team, we could excel. I could be courageous when necessary and often leaned on mentors to embrace conflict and learn from failures.

I learned early at SLG that this wasn't necessarily "my style" but that there was a foundation for my character and how I was leading. SLG gave me the language and a system that anyone can learn and make their own.

At SLG, we ground our leadership journey in virtues: love, integrity, truth, excellence, and relationships (LITER). While we all operate from a set of values, those values can and will change over time based on your circumstances. But virtues are tested, timeless, and transcendent.

For example, before becoming a mother, my values were vastly different. I was more daring and self-serving in my hobbies and interests. I valued individual bravery and challenging experiences like obtaining my pilot's license, traveling alone, and finding my way through foreign countries. At work, I spent hours training and supporting individuals on my team to help them improve so we could achieve superior results. I led with endless energy from the foundation of love, integrity, and truth, striving toward excellence (in experiences) and building relationships along the way.

Now, as a mother of two young boys, my values are more family and community-centered. My bravery may encompass speaking up at my sons' school and advocating for virtue-driven character leadership development. My challenging experiences include building relationships across generations, recruiting and training program participants, marketing to multiple audiences, and fundraising. I lead in this new backdrop with LITER because these revised values also require me to lead with love, integrity, truth, excellence, and relationships to create something great with the team.

At SLG, we also believe that growing in emotional intelligence is essential for great leaders. Emotional intelligence (EQ) is being aware of, controlling, expressing, and handling your emotions **and** understanding the emotions of others. A great leader realizes that understanding her emotions helps her better understand others and their emotions. EQ is a MUST-HAVE social skill for leaders and is critical for motivating others (for example, selling) or collaborating and harmonizing with others. The EQ elements of interpersonal relationships, empathy, and social responsibility connect closely to the behaviors we exhibit when leading with love. By increasing your ability to exercise those three areas of EQ, your leadership practice will grow in the virtue of love.

Prerequisite for Practice
1. Set aside some quiet time (15 minutes).
2. Agree to be open to self-reflection and introspection.
3. Permit yourself to practice the virtue of love.

The Nuts and Bolts

With paper and your favorite writing tool, find a quiet place and spend five minutes reflecting on time spent with close friends (like I did earlier) or the clients you know and appreciate the most. Write their names down (three to five people).

For the next five to ten minutes, try this exercise.

Draw three columns:

Label Column 1 "Rarely or Never."

Label Column 2 "Sometimes."

Label Column 3 "Often or consistently."

Down the left side of your paper, write the following ten **behaviors**. These behaviors are at the intersection of the EQ elements of interpersonal relationships, empathy, social responsibility, AND the virtue of love.

1. I am generous with my time and work to serve others.
2. I ask questions.
3. I listen.
4. I seek to inspire.
5. I aim to build the capacity of others.
6. I can challenge others when necessary.
7. I am willing to say no.
8. I display empathy and compassion.
9. I treat others with respect.
10. I believe in my friend, my customer, my client.

As you reflect on those you've chosen, ask yourself how often you exhibit the behaviors that tie to the virtue of love in leadership with them. Consider each behavior honestly and mark Columns 1, 2, or 3 to help you identify any behaviors that may be harder for you to practice.

Moving Forward

Did you find any surprises? I imagine you weren't surprised and know where you are not leading with your genuine love for others. Pick one behavior to work on daily over the next four weeks. Every morning for four weeks, remind yourself of your selected behavior (*I ask questions*). In the evening, review your day and draw a "heart" on your calendar if you've exercised that chosen behavior. After the four weeks, reflect on all the beautiful hearts and note what has changed in your business, team, and life as you've practiced this habit regularly.

Why is love a superpower in leadership? We are all created to be in relationship—to love and be loved by others. The way we lead is guided by character. Our character is revealed through our behaviors toward others. When we tap into our natural ability to love, the way we lead and our life is transformed.

Michael Leunig puts it simply in his poem: "Love and Fear."

There are only two feelings. Love and fear.

There are only two languages. Love and fear.

There are only two activities. Love and fear.

There are only two motives, two procedures, two frameworks, two results.

Love and fear.

Love and fear.

I encourage you to cast away your fear and lead with love. What will you choose?

Julie Campbell is a mother of two boys, wife to a college athletics coach, and President/CEO of the Severn Leadership Group (SLG), making the world a better place through virtuous leadership. She served for 20 years in the U.S. Navy in various leadership positions in space systems, electronic warfare, and communications, followed by ten years leading teams in the defense and information technology industries. With a passion and curiosity for people and their purposes, Julie is a life-long mentor and collaborator with a mission to help others level up their leadership as they change the world.

When she's not knee-deep in creating partnerships, fundraising, and growing the SLG network of mentors, fellows, and supporters, you can find her volunteering at her sons' school, cheering at sporting events, playing board games, or walking, listening to podcasts and reading (sometimes all three at once)! Julie relishes her precious time with her girlfriends. She prefers the beach over the mountains. And don't take her camping. Instead, offer her a sturdy roof over her head, a nice comfortable bed, good food, decent wine, and engaging company!

Connect with Julie at:

Website: https://www.severnleadership.org/
LinkedIn: https://www.linkedin.com/in/campbell-juliem/
Facebook: https://www.facebook.com/severnleadershipgroup
Instagram: https://www.instagram.com/slg_org/
Email: julie.campbell@severnleadership.org

Chapter 11

HOME SALES WITH HEART
My Story as a Community Realtor

Jennifer Guarnera Bonk, Real Estate Expert

MY STORY

My phone rings, and it's Wendy, the owner/operator of my Real Estate office, Keller Williams Flagship of Maryland. Wendy was calling to congratulate me. "You won! Top Team in both units and volume for the entire Maryland/DC region!" I was overwhelmed with gratitude and disbelief. Top Real Estate Team in the Maryland/DC Region. How did we get there? It had been a long road and lots of work to get us to this point. I was shocked. February 2022, I was sitting in the lobby of a Homewood Suites in Lancaster, Pennsylvania, with a bunch of moms and dads eating pizza and drinking wine, chatting and talking about our girls' field hockey games earlier that day. I couldn't believe it when I got Wendy's call and saw on my phone multiple messages of congratulations coming through. My husband, Kevin, and I decided to skip our yearly sales meeting for Keller Williams International to divide and conquer, supporting our kids that weekend. Missing the sales meeting meant missing this big announcement.

We often look at a moment of success, and for many, it might look like a good year or overnight achievement. The truth is that most success comes from years of dedication, implementation, and deliberate adjustments to maintain consistency and optimize our business. If we really want to talk about how we reached this success, we have to go back many years.

When my husband and I got married in 2001, I was teaching full-time, and he was a financial director for a company that managed properties all over the country. The county we lived in had a provisional teaching program that allowed me to teach while also earning my master's degree. While my undergrad was in communication disorders, an undergraduate program for speech pathology and audiology, through the provisional teaching program, I chose to obtain a master's degree in Special Education from Goucher College in Towson, Maryland. I did a brief stint as a teacher, specifically teaching high school special education. I found that I really connected with the high school-aged students. I had a lot of fun, felt I connected well with them and had great empathy and compassion for that age group. Some of the greatest things I gained from teaching were patience, problem-solving, organization, communication skills, and listening skills. My career as a teacher was fulfilling in so many ways.

Meanwhile, my family was growing. We had our first child in 2004, and after having our second child in 2006, I made a difficult decision to take time off from teaching to stay at home with my children. With my husband having a stable job and not feeling the pressure for me to contribute financially, we felt that it was best for our family for me to be home with our kids. I was excited for this next chapter in my life, and I was passionate about community and volunteerism, so even with young children, I was able to stay connected with the community. In January 2008, we were blessed with twins, growing our family to six with all four children under the age of four. Needless to say, life was suddenly very busy.

Kevin and I spent much of our early relationship dabbling in real estate. Even before we were married, he purchased a home to renovate. We had so much fun going through the process of flipping this home. To be young adults, making such big decisions, learning about the real estate market, and how to maximize the value of a property was exhilarating. We continued doing this as our young family was growing. My husband did the physical renovations and upgrades on properties, and I would tote babies around while picking out finishes and all the details. I was having so much fun being part of that process, and even with four young children, I saw how I could contribute to the family financially while still having flexibility. In December of 2008, I decided I wanted to get my real estate license because I thought it would be a job that was easy to do part-time and would offer flexibility.

Getting started as a realtor was really hard. I felt that no one wanted to help me. I was struggling to find clients and truly establish myself. I started with a traditional local broker and was assigned a mentor, but unfortunately, she was terrified to share any information with me because she saw me as a threat. I was still bright-eyed and bushy-tailed and felt a sense of professionalism and eagerness to get my business started. I did the best I could working the front desk in the office, hoping for someone to walk in looking for help or for the phone to ring with someone looking for representation for buying or selling their home. While I didn't really get to learn much from that experience, I felt a profound responsibility and a drive to achieve. I ran anywhere real estate took me. I jumped on any lead I could get. It was important to me that I built relationships with everyone I met because I knew that if I could build trust, I could build my business. As hard as I worked on building my business, I started to feel overwhelmed and undervalued. I was frustrated because I was beyond eager to learn and willing to do whatever it took to get clients.

Unfortunately, at home, we experienced financial difficulties. Kevin's employer had financial struggles and paid employees very sporadically. Suddenly, his once stable job was not so stable, and my part-time/flexible real estate work was now necessary. However, my business was new, and my income was next to nothing. Additionally, we had a contract for a year for an au pair to help care for our kids. The bills kept coming, and with our finances so inconsistent, we dug ourselves deeper and deeper into hundreds of thousands of dollars in debt. Kevin ultimately left that job, accepting a job with a family-owned real estate developer in Baltimore.

Around this time, I was recruited by a team in the Keller Williams office in Annapolis. Once I joined the team, I did my first deal, and then the learning really started. They had systems in place, providing team members the opportunity to build and grow. The environment fostered structure and accountability, and because I was finally working with clients, I received hands-on experience and training. The skills I gained as a teacher and as a community volunteer allowed me to shine.

I worked with the team for several months but soon realized I wanted to branch out on my own. I wanted to use my personal strengths and attributes to build a business that aligned with my values to help me create success. I have strong convictions and dedication to my values, and I knew there was something missing in how I wanted to build my business. The team leader in the office saw that I had potential and invested a lot of time to coach and guide me. She helped me discover my authentic business and leadership style and processes. This is where I discovered I could merge my passion for connection, community, and integrity into my real estate business.

Through coaching, I learned how to use my skills to further connect with my community. My real estate business was finally beginning to flourish, and I was starting to see that as I was building trust in the community, I was also cultivating more relationships, and that was ultimately leading to more business and sales. I found my groove and slowly started to see financial gain.

However, in December 2010, Kevin was laid off. I will never forget the moment he called me. I was driving down Route 40 in Ellicott City on my way to meet clients for drinks to discuss their upcoming move. Kevin was supposed to meet us for drinks as well. However, when he called, I could tell that he was truly upset. I felt crushed inside but knew I had to stay positive and uplifting for him. He had absolutely no idea how we were going to survive financially. Of course, Kevin was devastated; it was two weeks before Christmas, and we had four very young kids. I paused, and then I said something that absolutely stunned him.

"This is God's way of telling us you should work with me full-time. We'll take this time to come up with a plan and figure out how to make this work."

I built up my business enough so we were comfortable forgoing a salary, although 100% commission for both of us was a scary prospect. We knew we had an uphill climb, and we got right to work building our business.

Kevin has his MBA from the University of Maryland, and with his experience as a CPA (certified public accountant), he's very business savvy and great at spreadsheets and analysis. Naturally, he immediately became our paperwork, marketing, and social media specialist as well as our runner (basically meaning that he ran around and did all the manual labor for properties and setup). At that time, I was primarily the contact for clients. I managed all the showings and met with potential sellers. While it was exciting to be building our business together, we were still under a lot of stress. We struggled financially, had four young kids at home, and our marriage and personal relationship experienced some major shifts because we were with each other 24/7.

Working with your spouse isn't easy. We had a lot of learning to do. As we grew, we began to take on more clients. We experienced growing pains. While we discovered clearly defined strengths, we didn't have clearly defined roles. As we grew, our lanes began to blend, and at times, I became defensive about the business because I grew so much of it myself. It was hard to share. I wasn't always open to his ideas and changes, and he wasn't always open to how I wanted to grow and expand. In any partnership, it takes communication and compromise. After some therapy and bumps in the road, we found a way to support and complement each other's strengths, ideas, vision, and values.

We're often asked how we do all that we do with just the two of us. Juggling four teenagers and a seven-figure business is a lot for anyone. If you know us, you'll know we're basically a comedy. We've been told many times we should have our own TV show. If you see our life, our chaos can be quite startling. We're constantly running kids all over town to sports, school events, and social commitments. However, we've also raised four very independent teenagers because they've spent so much of their lives wrapped up in the fast-paced life of entrepreneurs. There was a lot of "drop a kid off, go show a house, swap kids at the next event, and grab dinner on your way to meet another client." Our life is chaos—organized chaos, but chaos, nonetheless. Thankfully, we're very lighthearted. We've been through a lot and have found that if we roll with the waves of life, we don't get sucked into the current.

With our full schedule between work, sports, and school, volunteering in our community is something I'm very deliberate about. We continue to stay modest, almost to a fault. If you ask anyone around us, I guarantee that unless they're very close to us, they have no idea of the volume our business does. I don't want to be flashy about the business we do. I want people to work with us because we're good people, not because we promise the highest sale. I have the confidence that I can do well for my clients, and I know I can do that with integrity, quality, and connection. My husband and I are constantly tag-teaming to make sure our clients never feel that we're stressed and overwhelmed by life or work. We seamlessly chauffeur children to sports while planning appointments, juggling paperwork, and whatever else needs to get done in between. It's very rare that one of us is not at our children's games or events. If you ask them, they'll tell you I'm around *too much*. Coincidentally (and even conveniently), we've had opportunities at mostly every extracurricular activity to network. Believe it or not, everyone wants to talk about real estate all the time.

Through the years, we've had other agents join our team. We helped multiple friends get their businesses up and going, and our team has had multiple "Rookies of the Year" within our brokerage. Ultimately, my husband and I decided we work best as a two-person team.

We've built our business to be community-based and hyper-local. We believe we can best service our buyers and sellers in areas we're personally familiar with. This has served us very well. Over 50% of our business is referral-based.

We feel very strongly about giving back to the community. We host multiple events throughout the year and open them to everyone in the community, not just past and current clients. We consistently have a Shred-It event in April, photos with the Easter Bunny and Santa, a Trunk-or-Treat event, and a movie night open to the whole community. We also hold a free pie night for past and current clients. I organize monthly women's events supporting small woman-owned businesses, providing an opportunity for networking.

Some would also call me a chronic volunteer. It's very important to me to give time and treasures to the different causes

I believe in. I often have my family participating right along with me, and I'm always looking for creative ways to give back to the local stores and restaurants while offering benefits to my clients.

Volunteering has always been important to me. I think if I could do that full-time, that's honestly what I'd do. I love the people I meet and that the focus is on the community. Being the introvert that I am, I don't necessarily have to talk about myself. I feel I'm doing something meaningful and impactful without any expectation of glory or recognition. I get to meet like-minded people, help my community, and feel I'm contributing in some small way.

What I've learned through my experience in volunteerism over the years is that while I worked hard and put in a lot of hours in various organizations, it was hard to connect, have meaningful relationships, and offer significant contributions when I was stretched too thin. I was frustrated that I was putting in so many hours but not able to connect with others, and I constantly felt like I could and should do more in each organization. Since I'm not a full-time volunteer as well as a mother of four—oh, and running my own business—doing more in so many organizations wasn't possible or realistic. We all have limited time and resources, and I knew I needed to gain clarity on where my time, talents, and treasures would best fit.

I took a hard look at what made the most sense in my life. I wanted to be part of something that would also be impactful to my kids. I think it's imperative for my kids to see how important volunteerism is and how it can affect different facets of their lives. I want to be sure they understand that even the smallest of actions can have a ripple effect on others.

One area of focus I chose was working with my children's school's PTA. My priority here was to really try to ensure the teachers felt valued, supported, and appreciated. Having a teaching background, I knew they sometimes felt underappreciated and burnt out. I know that while my kids might moan and groan and say how embarrassed they are to see me at the school, the lifelong lesson they gain is that teachers matter and we can give back in small ways that have big results. You don't have to go out and find some big organization. You can volunteer right where you are.

Another organization I directed my focus toward was fundraising and raising awareness for a local hospital in a low-income area where medical resources are limited. I learned about this organization nine years ago while I was at another fundraiser, and I was introduced to two ladies who were starting a group for young professionals at this hospital. I agreed to join their group, and after working with the group for years, I knew I wanted to do more. I learned so much about their various programs that I felt attached and invested in learning and doing more. The more I'm involved, the more passionate I become. This was an organization I'd been part of from the very beginning. It's been an incredible experience to watch ideas turn into projects, and it's been even more incredible to see those projects become pillars the community can depend on.

In learning to direct my focus on one or two organizations my family and I are passionate about, I now see we're able to make a greater impact overall. By having that focus, relationships become friendships, I learn more about myself and my community, feel like I'm going deeper (not wider) in my network, and the contributions feel more substantial.

Going back to that day in February, learning that Kevin and I received "Top Team" in Maryland and DC, I think about the connections we've made in our hometown, the example we've set for our children, and the friends and neighbors we've helped during important milestones in their lives. It's a reminder to me that, often, the relationship is worth more than the award and that when you trust yourself, live in alignment with your values, and truly bring people together, anything is possible.

THE PRACTICE

Let me explain what I mean when I say my network goes deeper, not wider. I've met some incredible people. It's inspiring to see how much they contribute through their volunteerism. These are people that see a need and act on it, and they do so selflessly as a true act of altruism. I often wonder if this act of selflessness comes naturally to most. It certainly makes me more mindful of my own actions. I'm inspired and motivated to continue to work on myself, and it makes me want to continue to surround myself with these types of people. I want to know more about them. I want to learn from them, and I want to be more like them. It makes me aware of my own self-perceptions and who I want to be part of my network. Your network isn't about how many people you know; it's about the quality of people you know.

How does network play into volunteerism? I believe that true marketing in your business really is personal and about your community, especially when you're talking about something as personal and important as buying and selling a home. When people say, "It's not personal; it's just business," I strongly disagree. I think our business is deeply personal, and I can only be effective and responsible in my business when I care about my clients and our community. Because I'm not an extroverted person, I find people trust me and value who I am as a person because they see the work I do in the community. I'm not shouting from the rooftops, "Look at me, I'll sell your house!" Rather, I'm quietly and diligently working to improve the circumstances around us. I work hard and value systems, processes, integrity, and ethics.

Have you ever heard the term "Marketing with a cause?" I truly believe in this model because I can really get behind it. I'm not promoting myself; I'm promoting my community, and I'm supporting other businesses in my community, thereby supporting my very own neighbors. For me, it was never about highest-ranking sales, accolades, and awards. It's always been about something bigger, contributing to my family and my community—something bigger than me. If I can help build a better place for us all to live, then I feel my true work has been accomplished.

Jennifer Bonk is an Anne Arundel County resident and proud mother. Jennifer and her husband, Kevin, have been successfully involved in investment real estate for over 15 years. Prior to becoming a licensed REALTOR®, Jennifer served as a high school special education teacher in the Anne Arundel County public schools system.

Jennifer specializes in buyer representation as well as listing and selling properties in Anne Arundel and the surrounding Counties. Jennifer has made the commitment to deliver the highest level of integrity and service. Referrals have become a major part of her business. If you are looking for a REALTOR® who uses the latest real estate technology to benefit both buyers and sellers, and if you live outside of Maryland, Jennifer would be happy to interview Realtors in your area to find you a great match.

Jennifer and her team prioritize the community that she lives in. Her team offers free activities open to anyone, including photos with Santa and the Easter bunny, neighborhood movie night with a free ice cream truck, and a Trunk or Treat for a safe trick-or-treating environment. It is a priority to make sure families of all socio-economics have access to fun, holiday-related activities. Jennifer is very involved in several volunteer groups, giving both in time and financially.

jenn@gotbonk.com
410-499-2251
https://gotbonk.kw.com/
https://www.facebook.com/gotbonk

Chapter 12

UNLOCKING THE POWER OF VULNERABILITY

Using Radical Authenticity to Amplify the Impact of Your Words

Camille Campins-Adams, BBA, MA, CEO of
WAY Media + Marketing

MY STORY

It was a sweltering June morning, made bearable only by the ocean breeze that relentlessly traveled its way toward me. I sat on a beach cabana in Juan Dolio, Dominican Republic–my family's new home, if only for summer break. My kids and I moved there for two months to be with my husband while he fulfilled a two-year contract that required him to work on the island. The condo's private beach or the balcony of our third-floor condo were the only places I could escape my three children and work peacefully while our brand new nanny, who didn't speak a word of English, cared for them.

On this noteworthy Thursday morning, I prepared for a call with my teammates, Shawna and Elizabeth. It was time to kick off our first six-figure book launch since opening WAY Media + Marketing for business in February, four short months earlier. As I prepared, I sat on that cozy cabana listening to Christian music. Suddenly, the song, *First Things First* by Consumed By Fire came on. I stopped everything to intentionally take in the lyrics: "First thing's first, I seek Your will, Not my own, Surrender all my wants to you."

I had listened to this song on repeat for months before this, crying through it a solid 50% of the time. It wasn't mere chance this particular song came on only ten minutes before our call was supposed to start. I quickly sent it to Shawna and Elizabeth via text, "Listen to this before our call if you can. I'm feeling called to do something different when we chat this morning." I felt strongly that I needed to run this call in a unique way, opening up my heart to the team and praying before we even got down to business. At that moment, those lyrics were exactly what I needed to ground myself and be reminded of why I started WAY in the first place.

As I opened the call with Shawna and Elizabeth, I started expressing what was on my heart. "WAY is not just a business to me; it's a calling. It's something God called me to do even when I didn't want to pursue it because of my own insecurities."

Starting a marketing agency was not my will, but I was certain it was His. Even though I was hesitant to walk by faith, taking one step at a time in the direction He was leading me, I knew

I had to be obedient. Through all the uncertainty and doubts creeping in, there was good news: I was very lucid about the fact that I wasn't called to do it alone. Not only was I not supposed to do it on my own, I would've never been able to experience the success I had without the two women I was locking eyes with on the other side of the computer screen. We all knew God ordained it from the very beginning, and we were blessed to be able to speak to it so openly on our call.

"I want to thank you both for being here and locking arms with me to build this company. Even though WAY is legally my business, my vision is to grow this together for the foreseeable future as *God's* business; not only would I not want to do this without you, this wouldn't be possible if it were not for Him and the two of you."

The floodgates opened, and tears started flowing down my face. As I poured my heart out, I kept trying to suppress the tears forcibly driving their way forward.

"My mom and sister are always telling me I'm too emotional and that I need to talk less and remain more guarded. 'Keep things to yourself as much as possible and don't talk about it,' they say."

Shawna stopped me, "No. Camille, you're someone people want to be around because you *are* so open and vulnerable. You're real with how you feel, and it's refreshing in a world of inauthenticity and hidden agendas."

Elizabeth chimed in, "I agree. Your vulnerability leads by example. We can't help people bravely share their story in a memoir if we aren't capable of radical authenticity ourselves. We lead by example. We show them the way."

Although WAY seemed to have sprung up overnight, my path to becoming an entrepreneur was anything but short and sweet. The roots I planted go way back to a time when I barely saw myself as a writer. It took a lot of courage and vulnerability to own the title of writer and–eventually–writing coach. And even then, I thought I found my *thing* with book coaching, but my path ultimately led me toward helping authors get their books out into the world in a big WAY. That's when I had to find the courage again to expand outside my comfort zone, becoming a book launch strategist and founding a marketing agency for authors.

What I discovered along my journey is the value of getting outside your comfort zone. Because the reality is, everything we've ever wanted is just outside that safe little bubble we protect ourselves with. I also learned to embrace writing as much more than just a means of expression; it's a journey of self-discovery, healing, and immense growth if you allow it to be. The act of putting your uncensored thoughts on paper is transformative, and it should be embraced more often as a powerful tool for personal growth. Whether you're driven to write a book for mass distribution, share a powerful testimony, or simply process your thoughts and feelings, the benefits of writing with radical authenticity are immeasurable.

As a writing coach, I've had the privilege of working with writers of all kinds, guiding them to understand the profound benefits of writing. The journey of embracing vulnerability and forming a consistent writing practice is unique to each individual– as unique as all the reasons one may be called to write. Many of us come to writing because we have a profound need to share the words that live deep in our souls. Some of us have been told we really should write a book because our life experiences can serve as a powerful testimony, while others explore writing simply for the therapeutic benefits. Regardless of where our motivations lie, we must remember that, as humans, we all have something real and raw to say, and writing is a powerful way to share our truth. Your truth may become a book one day, or it may remain tucked into a leather-bound notebook. Either is fine.

When I first felt the pull to write a book, I had no idea what that was or what it looked like. Something bigger than me just told me I had to write; I had to create. I was called for this— whatever *this* was. The first words I ever playfully wrote as an aspiring author were written in an embossed, blue suede leather-bound journal right after I graduated college. To this day, that journal has never seen the light of day.

For years, I knew I wanted to write, and yet I still didn't take my writing seriously. It wasn't until the spring of 2012, as a twenty-four-year-old newlywed, that something changed. I found myself up late one night surfing the internet. I sat on a bar stool, my body perched up on the kitchen counter of the cozy 1,000-square-foot cottage my husband David and I rented in Coconut Grove, Florida. Our Labrador mix and three black cats were sleeping close by, always keeping me company in David's absence as he spent months away playing professional baseball.

I honestly don't remember my exact reasons for being on the computer that night, but I do know it was at that moment that I decided I wanted to start documenting my life as a baseball wife in written format—an online diary of sorts. As I sat in my kitchen that beautiful South Florida evening in 2012, I came across the blog of another baseball wife. I was instantly drawn to the author's candidness, and I knew in my bones that I needed to start taking writing more seriously. I would start by writing about baseball too. That little blog of mine ended up taking off, syndicated by MLBlogs, and I found myself being thanked over and over again for being so honest and real about what being a baseball wife actually looked like. It wasn't uncommon to get Twitter replies saying things like, "Yes! Thank you for speaking up about this. There are so many challenges with this lifestyle, and I appreciate you opening up about the reality of it." Fueled by remarks like these, it didn't take long for me to realize how writing in a vulnerable, authentic way could impact the lives of others in a positive way.

A few years later, shortly after David retired from playing baseball and transitioned into coaching, I decided to go back to school to get a master's in creative writing. At the time, my oldest was three years old, and my youngest was not quite two. It was a crazy time to attempt to go back to school while also going back to work, but that wouldn't stop me.

While in graduate school, I set out to write a memoir as my thesis. That experience was grueling but also an incredibly cathartic process. I poured my soul onto the page time and time again, even though it proved to be painful. The truth is, writing about your life is hard, but what's most challenging is tearing your chest wide open and exposing yourself to the world. If there's one thing I learned in grad school, it's that readers will smell disingenuous writing. They can sense when the author is holding back. Hearing from my professors that my writing was great but that they knew I wasn't telling the whole truth was hard to swallow. When I started the process, I didn't realize writing a memoir would be so emotionally challenging.

I took their recommendations to heart, and in a few short months, I went from writing only the details I felt comfortable and safe sharing to exposing myself in ways that made me squirm. This was an important lesson I had to learn as a writer and marketer; where we forge bonds and connections with other people is not in the safe zone. Rather, true connections are cultivated when we become vulnerable and uncomfortable. The best writers–those who impact lives in a big way–are willing to bear it all for the sake of the truth–both (t)ruth and (T)ruth.

Before I delve deeper into the power of vulnerability, it's crucial to distinguish between two types of truth: Big T Truth (absolute truth) and Little t Truth (relative truth). Big T Truth represents the timeless and universally valid principles that hold steadfast regardless of perspective or context. These absolute truths are the bedrock of our existence. On the other hand, Little t truth comprises subjective, contextual truths shaped by personal experiences, beliefs, and emotions. They vary from person to person and can change over time. As writers, we must honor both types of truth, acknowledging that every book worth reading touches on at least one universal truth that resonates deeply with readers.

As writers, we must remember that vulnerability is a powerful way to connect with readers on a deep and profound level. Our truths, whether shared in a book or kept in a private journal, hold immense value and are worthy of being expressed. We must embrace vulnerability as a superpower and unleash our words and insights, knowing that the act of writing itself is a transformative and empowering journey.

As I sat on the cabana on that humid June morning, tears streaming down my cheeks, I couldn't help but reflect on the significance of vulnerability in my life and in the work we did at WAY Media + Marketing. Vulnerability is not just some abstract concept; it's a profound and universal Big T Truth we all grapple with, whether we realize it or not.

Big T Truth: Vulnerability is an inherent aspect of the human experience.

From the very moment we take our first breath to the final moments of our lives, vulnerability is woven into the fabric of our existence. It's in the way we love deeply, knowing our hearts might be broken. It's in the way we pursue our dreams, knowing that failure and disappointment are possible outcomes. It's in the way we open ourselves up to others, knowing we might be rejected or misunderstood. Vulnerability is not just a fleeting emotion; it's a fundamental part of what it means to be human.

Big T Truth: Vulnerability is the foundation of genuine connections.

In that tearful moment, I understood that my ability to be open, honest, and vulnerable with Shawna and Elizabeth, and their willingness to reciprocate it, was what made our relationship so strong. Our clients and authors gravitated toward us because they sensed our authenticity. It was not just about marketing strategies and book launches; it was about forming meaningful connections with people who trusted us to share their stories with the world.

Looking back on my journey with WAY Media + Marketing, I realized that vulnerability was the key to the powerful connections we formed with our clients and authors. When we allowed ourselves to be open and honest, we created spaces where others felt safe to do the same. Our vulnerability became a bridge that connected us with people on a profound level, transcending the superficial and allowing us to touch their lives in meaningful ways.

Big T Truth: Vulnerability breeds empathy and inspires others to do the same.

In a world that often encourages us to wear masks and hide our true selves, embracing vulnerability is a radical act of courage. When we share our authentic stories, struggles, and triumphs, we invite others to do the same. Vulnerability begets vulnerability, and in this cycle of openness, we find empathy and understanding that unite us as human beings.

Big T Truth: Vulnerability is a sign of strength and authenticity.

There's a misconception that vulnerability is a sign of weakness, but I've come to realize that it takes immense strength to be vulnerable. It's not easy to confront our fears, insecurities, and past wounds. Yet, in doing so, we showcase our authenticity and create spaces where others can feel safe to be themselves. Vulnerability is not a flaw to be hidden; it's a beacon of our true selves shining brightly.

Big T Truth: Vulnerability leads to personal and professional growth.

Throughout my journey as a writer, marketer, and business owner, I've experienced firsthand how embracing vulnerability leads to growth and transformation. When we're willing to step outside our comfort zone and share our unfiltered truths, we create opportunities for self-discovery and personal development.

Vulnerability is the catalyst that propels us toward becoming the best version of ourselves.

Vulnerability is not merely a passing lesson from my past; it stands as an eternal Big T Truth that continues to shape my life and the very core of WAY Media + Marketing. Embracing vulnerability is not always a smooth path, but it remains an indispensable aspect of our humanity—a force that enriches our connections, magnifies our impact, and unlocks doors to both personal and professional growth.

As I reflect on my journey and the profound impact of vulnerability, I stand firm in the belief that sharing our stories, struggles, and truths with radical authenticity is akin to unleashing a superpower. By embracing vulnerability, we inspire others to follow suit, forging authentic connections and fostering an atmosphere of openness and understanding.

So, dear reader, as you embark on your writing journey or any endeavor in life, I encourage you to embrace vulnerability as your ally. Let it be your guiding light, a powerful tool that touches the hearts of your readers, leaving a lasting impact. Just like the great writers whose works touch on universal truths, find the courage to tap into the Big T Truths of vulnerability—those timeless principles that resonate with every human soul.

Remember, you're not alone in this journey. Every book worth reading uncovers at least one universal truth that binds us together as a collective human experience. By sharing your words and insights with vulnerability, you become part of this tapestry that connects us all. Your stories matter, and your willingness to be vulnerable opens doors to understanding, empathy, and transformation.

So, as you write and share, do so with the spirit of authenticity and courage. Embrace vulnerability as your superpower and create a world where genuine connections and heartfelt stories have the power to change lives. Let our words be a testament to the incredible impact of vulnerability, uniting us in the pursuit of truth and human connection. Embrace vulnerability, and let it lead you to a place where your words resonate, inspire, and leave an indelible mark on the hearts of others.

THE PRACTICE

In this chapter, we've explored the power of vulnerability and its role as a superpower in our lives and creative pursuits. We've recognized the difference between Big T Truths (absolute truths) and Little t truths (relative truths) and how vulnerability connects us through shared experiences. Now it's time to take action and implement practical tools that will enable you to embrace vulnerability in your writing and personal journey.

Tool 1: Journaling with Radical Authenticity

Journaling is a powerful tool to connect with our inner selves and explore our vulnerabilities in a safe and private space. Create a journaling practice where you commit to writing with radical authenticity. Set aside time each day or week to reflect on your experiences, emotions, and thoughts. Be honest and open with yourself, acknowledging your fears, insecurities, and dreams. Embrace vulnerability on these pages, knowing that no one else will read them. Through this practice, you'll cultivate a deeper understanding of yourself and gain insights that can inspire your writing and personal growth.

Tool 2: Writing Vulnerability Letters

Incorporate vulnerability letters into your writing practice. Choose a person you trust as the recipient. You can even write these letters to yourself. In these letters, express your feelings, vulnerabilities, and truths without reservation. These letters serve as a means of processing emotions, healing past wounds, and fostering a sense of self-compassion. You can choose to send these letters to the intended recipient or keep them for your personal growth. Either way, the act of writing vulnerability letters can be liberating and transformative.

Tool 3: Seek Connection through Storytelling

Incorporate vulnerability into your storytelling. Whether you're writing fiction or nonfiction, create characters or narratives that resonate with real human experiences. Share authentic moments and emotions, allowing readers to connect with your work on a profound level. By weaving vulnerability into your stories, you create a space for readers to relate, empathize, and find solace in the shared human experience.

Tool 4: Embrace Feedback with Openness

As you share your writing with others, embrace feedback with an open heart and mind. Understand that vulnerability opens you up to critique, but it also creates opportunities for growth. Be receptive to constructive criticism and use it as a catalyst for improvement. Embracing vulnerability in this way allows you to develop as a writer and embrace the journey of continuous learning and refinement.

Tool 5: Connect with a Supportive Community

Surround yourself with a supportive community that values vulnerability and encourages authentic sharing. Seek writing groups, workshops, or online communities where individuals share their creative journeys openly and support one another. Engaging with like-minded individuals who understand the power of vulnerability can be empowering and uplifting, fueling your creativity and sense of belonging.

Tool 6: Practice Vulnerable Speaking

Extend vulnerability beyond writing and into your spoken communication. Embrace vulnerability when speaking about your experiences and sharing your thoughts and insights. Whether it's through public speaking engagements, discussions with friends, or networking events, practice being open and authentic with your words. Vulnerable speaking allows you to connect with others on a deeper level, fostering genuine relationships and building trust.

Tool 7: Celebrate Vulnerability Milestones

Recognize and celebrate your vulnerability milestones along the way. Every time you embrace vulnerability and share your truth, no matter how big or small, acknowledge your courage and growth. Celebrate each step you take toward living authentically, writing fearlessly, and embracing vulnerability as a superpower.

As you integrate these actionable tools into your writing and personal journey, remember that vulnerability is not a destination but a continuous process of growth and connection. Embrace vulnerability as your superpower, knowing it holds the potential to amplify the impact of your words and create meaningful connections with readers and the world. Trust in the power of your authentic voice, and let it guide you toward a life of radical authenticity, personal growth, and storytelling that touches hearts and changes lives. Embrace vulnerability and embark on a transformative journey toward becoming the best version of yourself through the power of writing and radical authenticity.

Camille Campins-Adams is a writing coach, book launch strategist, and speaker on a mission to empower women to embody their best selves through the transformative power of writing. With a profound belief in vulnerability as a superpower, Camille guides individuals to unleash their authentic voices and make their dreams a reality.

With years of experience in the writing industry, Camille understands the profound impact of sharing our stories with radical authenticity. She knows that writing goes beyond mere words on paper; it's a conduit for personal growth, self-discovery, and forging genuine connections with others.

As a dedicated writing coach, Camille provides personalized support to aspiring writers, helping them navigate the creative process with confidence. She encourages her clients to embrace their vulnerability, empowering them to share their stories fearlessly and make a meaningful impact on readers.

As the CEO and Founder of WAY Media + Marketing, Camille knows the strategic steps to turn dreams into reality. She guides authors in successfully launching their books, amplifying their reach and message to touch the hearts of a wider audience.

A captivating motivational speaker, Camille's talks inspire audiences with insights on courage, vulnerability, and the transformative power of words. Her engaging and transparent approach invites others to step into their power and create positive change in their lives and the lives of those around them.

Visit CamilleCampinsAdams.com to embark on a transformative journey toward a life enriched by the power of vulnerability and storytelling.

Connect with Camille on social media:

Website: https://CamilleCampinsAdams.com
Facebook: https://www.Facebook.com/CamilleCampinsAdams
Instagram: https://www.Instagram.com/CampinsAdams
LinkedIn: https://www.linkedin.com/in/camille-campins-adams/

Chapter 13

SMASH YOUR SCALE

Improve Your Whole Health by Shifting Your Focus from Weight to Wellbeing

Elizabeth Harris, MS, RDN,
Certified Intuitive Eating Counselor

MY STORY

Doing complicated chemistry and food science experiments in my kitchen while cooking dinner, helping three kids finish their homework, and navigating the pre-dinner witching hour is not my idea of a good time. And yet, I spent a lot of very stressful hours over several years doing exactly that.

Why on Earth would I do such a thing?

Even though I studied the Russian language in college (that wasn't as useful in the post-Cold War 1990s as it sounds today) and then worked for a while editing, marketing, and copywriting financial publications, I realized later in life that the things that light me up the most are food, nutrition, and promoting wellness. So, after considering it for a long time, I finally decided to follow my passion and switch careers in my 40s. I wanted to become a dietitian so I could help people improve their health through better food choices and healthy habits. As it turns out, it's not that easy to become a dietitian when you're well-versed in Russian literature, the Cyrillic alphabet, and the history of tsars and Soviet Republics, but not the periodic table or the citric acid cycle.

I needed to make my way through 13 pre-requisite undergraduate science classes just to *get into* the master's level nutrition and dietetics program. Truthfully, I hemmed and hawed over making this overwhelming leap for so long that I had to repeat one of the classes because it expired before I was ready to apply to dietetics programs! Once I got underway, though, I could only take most of these classes sequentially, one semester at a time, so it took me several years to finish them all. I was a stay-at-home mom by then, which meant I had to fit the courses in around my kids' school, sports, playdates, and our other family activities. Enter the seemingly never-ending chemistry labs in my kitchen, dinnertime and late-night food science experiments, and anatomy models on my coffee table.

Eventually, *thankfully*, I applied and accepted into a distance learning program at the University of Southern California. That's when the stress—ahem, I mean the fun— began. You know that movie, *The Internship*, with Vince Vaughn and Owen Wilson, where two midlife, fish-out-of-water salesmen intern at Google? That was me. A forty-plus-year-old woman with three pre-teens and teens running herself ragged in a full-time master's program that combined the coursework and dietetic internship requirements all in one. So not only was I a full-time student, but I was simultaneously working my way through eight different internship rotations, sometimes with supervisors who were half my age. It was fascinating, overwhelming, and extremely humbling.

Then, things took a rather unexpected turn.

The Abrupt Pivot

As a new dietitian who had just been trained in a traditional, weight-centric model of nutrition and health, I set out to open a private nutrition coaching practice aimed at helping people improve their eating habits and health. Like many colleagues before and after me, I assumed this would need to center around helping people lose weight. After all, that's what dietitians do and what many people who are ready to prioritize their nutrition and health are looking for and need, *right*?

For a hot second, I worked with clients whose primary goal was weight loss. But to be honest, I hated it. Something within me just didn't feel right about making weight the focal point of my work or people's health. By this point, I had three teenagers, two girls and a boy. Far too many people close to us were struggling with disordered eating and eating disorders. *My business is all over social media*, I thought. *My kids, their friends, and many of our loved ones see the things I share about food and bodies, along with everyone else. What's the most helpful, healthful message I can put in front of them?* Like the rest of us, teens are immersed in toxic diet culture, and they're also especially susceptible to harmful and unrealistic social media ideals about thinness and beauty. Teens are by no means the only people who suffer from eating disorders, but it all just seemed to be hitting too close to home. I couldn't comfortably bring myself to promote weight loss and dieting when I knew how many people in our orbit had fragile relationships with food and their bodies.

Most people don't fully understand this, but dieting behaviors are often disordered eating behaviors in disguise that get inadvertently reinforced when people are praised for weight loss. Also, dieting can be a precursor to the development of full-blown eating disorders. Throw in the fact that our cultural obsession with thinness and weight makes it nearly impossible for *practically anyone* to feel confident and comfortable with their bodies, and perhaps you'll understand why I wanted something more and better for my kids and everyone else too.

As a new entrepreneur in a profession where most people expect you to play a role in so-called weight management, not wanting to focus on weight loss or weigh my clients put me in a bit of a pickle. And yet, my gut kept steering me away: *Bodies naturally come in all shapes and sizes. Weight and health are not the same thing.* Looking back, thank goodness it did because I now understand how harmful weight-centered approaches can be.

There was something else, too. I noticed my weight loss clients could be making all sorts of incredibly helpful changes to their nutrition and eating habits that had them feeling good. But if they stepped on the scale and didn't like the number they saw, all their good feelings and positive momentum immediately vanished. They'd inevitably start beating themselves up, questioning their bodies or their efforts, wondering what they were doing wrong or why they were even bothering. "Elizabeth," they'd say, "it's not working."

This made me sad. The truth was that they were working hard to make positive, meaningful changes to their eating and exercise routines. I had no doubt these changes would benefit their health. *Of course, it's "working,"* I'd think. And yet the scale was so often a trigger for people to question their efforts, want to give up, or be mean and punishing to themselves.

There must be a better way to support people's eating, health, and well-being than focusing on weight loss.

To echo Ross from *Friends*, even though I'd barely begun, it was time to pivot and ask myself some hard questions. *What is health? What does it look like to eat healthfully? How can I best support my clients to prioritize their nutrition, improve their health, and feel good in their bodies?*

The Shocking Findings

I was already well-versed in the typical weight-centered approaches to nutrition and health. So instead, I threw myself into the research behind Intuitive Eating, an evidence-based, *weight-neutral* approach to nutrition and health that emphasizes dropping out of diet culture, having a happy, healthy relationship with food, and focusing on health-promoting behaviors rather than weight.

What I found next blew me away. If I'm being honest, I had a hard time at first accepting what I learned.

How can this be true? It contradicts so much of what I've been taught about weight and health. Why aren't more people talking about this? Why are SO many people saying something so very different?

For the sake of brevity, here is the Cliff Notes version of some of what I learned. I need to share this with you for you to understand the life-changing shift I was about to make; plus, the word needs to get out:

- Dieting (in all its many forms) may lead to *short-term* weight loss, but the results rarely last, with some studies pegging the long-term failure rate as high as a whopping 95%.[1]
- Not only does dieting seldom result in sustainable weight loss, but there's a lot of high-quality research demonstrating that dieting often leads to *weight gain* over time.[2]
- The repeated weight loss and gains that so often accompany dieting, what's called weight cycling, has been linked with negative health outcomes independent of body size, including twice the normal risk of heart disease and higher rates of overall mortality.[3, 4]
- The body mass index (BMI) is a deeply flawed and unreliable proxy for health, and the raw data likely don't even show what you'd expect. For example, there's a large (and ever-growing) body of research showing that the BMI category classified as "underweight" is linked with the highest risk of mortality, while being classified as "overweight" may be *protective* for longevity.[5,6] *Yes, you really did read that correctly!*
- While we know that "obesity" is linked with poorer health outcomes, we cannot prove that being at a higher weight *causes* those illnesses. Correlation does not equal causation, and the variables impacting health outcomes

are multifaceted. We know, for example, that people in larger bodies suffer from cultural weight stigma, a form of chronic stress. We also know that individuals who experience discrimination in its many unfortunate forms have higher rates of poorer physical and mental health outcomes. Also—*and this is important*—many of the health conditions that get attributed to body size are also linked with weight stigma itself, yet that's rarely talked about.[7]

- There's more. We also know that individuals in larger bodies experience anti-fat bias in medical settings too, which can delay or deter them from seeking out care and negatively impact the quality of care they receive. This, too, negatively impacts health outcomes and muddies the research on weight and health (the effects of weight stigma are rarely controlled for in scientific studies).

- You're probably familiar with the many studies that show improvements in certain health markers with weight loss. But in the majority of these studies, people are changing their eating, exercise, or other lifestyle behaviors to achieve that (often temporary) weight loss. This means we can't say for sure if it's the weight loss *per se* that's responsible for those improvements or if it's the change in behaviors. Evidence shows we can improve health outcomes with supportive behavior change, regardless of whether it results in weight loss.[8,9]

With the accepted truths about weight and health now very much called into question in my mind, I dove deeper, getting acquainted with toxic diet culture. In a nutshell, it's a system of beliefs equating thinness with health, superiority, and moral virtue that's woven into the very fabric of our lives. I think of diet culture as the lens through which we all see food, health, and having a body—and boy is it a misshapen lens with a very narrowly defined and accepted body "ideal."

What the actual what? Everything I thought I knew has just been turned roundly on its ear. What if we've been going about this health thing all wrong? What if the traditional weight-centered approach causes more harm than good? What if there's a more effective way to help people eat better and improve their health—and it includes educating people on the harms of focusing on weight and weight loss, as well as challenging noxious diet culture?

My mind spun for weeks and weeks. It felt subversive. And daunting.

I'm an introvert. Pretty shy. I like to fade away in a crowd.

Could I really go out, *publicly*, with such a swimming-against-the-tide message? Could I really join the movement, started long ago by many brave, smart, and much more capable people than me, fighting against toxic diet culture, weight bias, and all its many, many harms?

I thought about all those amazing people I knew personally who were struggling with eating disorders. I thought about clients, friends, and family who had battled their weight for much of their lives. I thought about the lengths they were willing to go to in the name of weight loss and the frustration and desperation that the ups and downs of dieting had caused them, along with the tremendous toll it all took on their body image, self-worth, and self-esteem.

I thought about how much of our collective time, money, and energy is spent thinking about and fearing food—counting, tracking, and measuring portion sizes, doing all sorts of mental gymnastics to avoid eating so-called junk food, battling cravings, or forcing down unnecessary, bogus detoxes. I thought about all the people who have used exercise as a punishment for eating or who are obsessed with the number of calories they earn or burn in the gym. I thought about all the people who suffer from the devasting effects of fatphobia. All the people in smaller bodies who are still chasing weight loss, never feeling as though their bodies are good enough just as they are.

I reflected on my own body insecurities. I remembered that I was so uncomfortable with the idea of gaining weight or my body changing after pregnancy that I exercised like a fiend up until the day I delivered. I put so much pressure on myself to get back into the gym as soon as humanly possible after my babies were born because I desperately wanted to get my "pre-baby" body back. Why? Shouldn't I have been resting and healing? Celebrating what my body had just accomplished? Was it so unacceptable for my body to change *after birthing three humans?* At the time, people praised my dedication, but I now know what I had was a disordered relationship with exercise and a body image in need of healing. I thought about all the conversations I had with girlfriends, lamenting our weight or bashing our bodies, fearing the changes already happening with perimenopause.

There's so much unnecessary, *unhealthful* stress. My heart still breaks when I think about all the guilt and shame the obsession with weight, shape, and body size breeds.

And then I got mad.

Diet culture robs us of the joy of eating, moving, or caring for our bodies. And to be clear, since we're nearly all ensnared in the *culture* of dieting and the fixation on thinness, we don't even have to be dieters for the pressure to take a stranglehold on us! Essentially, diet culture keeps us all stuck, constantly thinking *about* our bodies instead of living life to the fullest *in* our bodies.

Challenge Accepted

So, my answer was a resounding (albeit a vulnerable) YES. Yes, I *would* join the anti-diet movement centered on unmasking diet culture, challenging weight stigma, and promoting and providing respectful, weight-neutral care for all people in all bodies. I *would* advocate for a better way to promote holistic health—and I *would* support people to nurture theirs more effectively. I *needed* to.

First, I had to home in on my answer to those three questions I posed earlier. What is health? What is healthy eating, *really*? And how would I best support my clients, knowing what I now did?

Truthfully, there are as many answers to the first question as there are individuals. But for me, the answer that I came up with is this. Health is the sweet spot where one's physical, mental, and emotional wellbeing, what I like to call whole health, is nurtured and supported.

When it comes to *healthy eating*, given that diet culture's version is so distorted, what should it look like? Intuitive Eating helped me realize that, as a culture and as traditional health experts, we're so busy prescriptively telling people what to eat, or more typically, fearmongering about what *not* to eat, that we've forgotten that *how* people eat is just as important to their overall health and wellbeing.

So, for me, healthy eating means, first and foremost, having a happy, healthy relationship with food. It means eating foods you love, without guilt or shame, in ways that taste good, feel good, and support your body's nutritional *and emotional* needs. It includes lots of nutrient-dense foods and plenty of fun foods too.

Importantly, trying to eat healthfully shouldn't drain your soul, as so often happens. Rather, it should be enjoyable, feel good, and enrich the quality of your life.

My Recipe for Whole Health and Wellbeing

Here's where my pivotal shift landed me. My mission is to help people reimagine their relationship with food, movement, and their bodies, gently transforming their approach to nutrition, whole health, and self-care.

My Whole Health Manifesto goes a little something like this. Eat foods you love *without guilt or shame*. Honor your hunger, fullness, and other innate eating cues. Choose nourishing foods in amounts that feel good in your unique body. Whenever possible, gently *add in* nutrient-dense foods rather than focusing on foods to restrict, eliminate, or avoid. Move regularly, as much as you are able, in ways that please you. Sleep. Spend quality time with friends and loved ones. Prioritize enjoyable and supportive self-care that helps you manage and recover from stress. Respect your here-and-now body, and remember that your size does not determine your worth or value.

Add a dash of gratitude, self-compassion, and curiosity. Listen and respond to your body, adjust as needed, and repeat. It's a lifelong *practice*, which means you can't get it wrong. There's no failure when it comes to caring for or nourishing your body— only helpful feedback.

Trust yourself. Trust your body.

Helping people rebuild trust in their bodies and their food choices with a more gentle, inclusive approach to nutrition and health is one of the most rewarding parts of my work. Not only is it an all-around whole health win, but it enables them to show up so much more authentically and empowered in all the other areas of their lives too.

THE PRACTICE

After working to help hundreds of individuals reimagine their relationship with food and body, here's what I know. Shifting the narrative from self-control to self-care with Intuitive Eating is a powerful, life-changing paradigm that helps people find peace with food and their bodies and transform how they approach nutrition and health.

Step one on the path to prioritizing your whole health is dropping out of toxic diet culture. To do so, I need to help you understand more fully what it is and how it shows up in your life.

Diet culture is a $255 *billion* industry that, to my mind, is synonymous with pressure[10]. Pressure to eat a certain way, pressure to exercise a certain way, and pressure to look a certain way. In their fabulous book, *Burnout*, Amelia and Emily Nagoski refer to it as "Big Bikini," an unfortunate nod to Big Pharma or Big Tobacco that perfectly captures how powerful and pervasive the massive industry has become. And make no mistake, while it may be masked under the guise of health, diet culture is ultimately about profits. There are a lot of people making a lot of money off seeding and then offering a "solution" to body-based insecurities.

As breathtaking as that hundreds of billion-dollar figure is, most people are still shocked to learn how very deep and ingrained diet culture is in our collective psyche. It's so much bigger and more insidious than keto, Atkins, Weight Watchers, Noom, or any other specific diet you can think of. As I said earlier, you don't have to be a dieter for diet culture to derail your efforts at feeling good about food and your body or to impact the way you view health and yourself.

Diet culture is a deeply ingrained belief system that promotes thinness as the gateway to happiness, health, comfort, individual worth, and more, often at the expense of physical, mental, and emotional wellbeing. Diet culture attaches moral value to food and ways of eating, labeling some foods and eaters as "good" or "virtuous" and others as "bad" or "junk." It equates thinness with health even though they're not the same thing. Healthy bodies can and do come in all shapes and sizes.

Diet culture shows up when you:

- hear a group of friends lamenting their weight, body shape, or size.
- hear or talk about being "good" for eating certain foods or "cheating" for choosing others.
- feel guilty for eating certain foods.
- are encouraged to earn or burn calories through exercise.
- assume being thin is key or equivalent to being healthy.
- see certain body shapes, sizes, and types promoted as the "ideal" to strive for.
- come across the myriad of diets, "lifestyle changes," or "wellness plans" that are just diets in disguise.
- encounter before and after weight loss images.
- experience or face weight or body shaming, weight stigma, or fatphobia.
- see or feel the need for weight loss supplements, teas, books, and products.
- encounter weight stigma in medical settings.

There are bunches of other examples, but I'm guessing you get the idea. Diet culture is toxic and pervasive. The analogy I like to share for protecting yourself is this. Unfortunately, we're all stuck in the swirling storm of diet culture. We may not be able to change the weather, but we can make sure we have the right gear to survive the storm.

Here are some steps you can take today to shelter yourself from the harms of diet culture.

First, commit to stop dieting or chasing weight loss. The research is clear that it doesn't work, and I've shown you many of the ways that it causes harm. Just remember that diet culture is sneaky; it's constantly shapeshifting because more and more people are realizing that diets are ineffective. Not every diet will be clearly labeled as such. They may be billed as wellness plans, lifestyle changes, clean eating programs, or something similar, but if the goal is weight loss through calorie restriction or micromanagement, it's a diet.

Second, unsubscribe from all things diet culture. Turn off radio and TV advertisements centered on weight loss or dieting. Unfollow, block, or mute accounts or people on social media who promote weight loss products, diets, and before and after images, or anyone who fear-mongers about food, weight, or health. Throw out your diet books and calorie-counting apps or tools, and cancel your weight loss subscriptions or memberships.

Ask yourself this simple question: Does this person, program, tool, conversation, or account make me feel better or worse about my body or more or less easeful around food? If it's the latter, do what you can to block it.

When it comes to social media, the more you unfollow, block, and mute diet culture accounts, the less of them the algorithms will show you, especially if you replace them with Intuitive Eating, weight-neutral, and body-positive accounts.

Third, smash your scale, or at the very least, put it away and out of sight. I know this may sound crazy or perhaps even impossible, and I get what you're feeling. But it's possible to live a long and healthful life without knowing your weight. Trust me when I tell you, it's much more peaceful too.

Ask yourself honestly what impact the scale has on you. Do you hyper-monitor the scale daily? Does the number you see impact your mood or how you feel about yourself?

Does it change or dictate the tone of your day or influence what you eat or how you move?

For example, if you see a number you like, are you more likely to give yourself a break and to "cheat" with your food choices? Conversely, if you don't like the number you see, do you wonder why you're even bothering to try to shift your eating or exercise more? Do you start berating yourself or your body? If so, I'm sorry to tell you that the scale is likely undermining your health and wellbeing.

If you don't feel ready to break up with the scale permanently, try cutting back on how often you weigh yourself slowly. Instead of weighing in daily, try for every other day at first and then wean yourself down to weekly, monthly, and perhaps eventually, never.

Finally, remind yourself loudly and often that you are here to experience and impact the world, not to decorate it. Also, health and weight are not the same thing. *As I share with my clients, healthful behaviors may not result in weight loss, but they're still health-promoting!*

Elizabeth Harris is a registered dietitian, certified Intuitive Eating counselor, speaker, entrepreneur, and co-host of the podcast Wellness Rebranded. She's passionate about empowering people to drop out of diet culture and reimagine their relationship with food, movement, and their bodies so they can prioritize their whole health with Intuitive Eating, gentle nutrition, and body image healing.

Known for her self-compassion, gentleness, and non-judgmental approach, along with her undying love of dark chocolate peanut butter cups, Elizabeth's motto is "self-care, not self-control." Because food is meant to be enjoyed, movement should make you happy, and we've all got better things to do than counting carbs or calories!

Elizabeth holds a Master's degree in Nutrition, Healthspan, and Longevity from the University of Southern California and a Bachelor's degree in Russian language and Slavic and East European Studies from the University of Connecticut. In her spare time, you'll find her keeping backyard bees, gardening, reading voraciously, and traveling the world with her husband and three teenagers—hitting every available farmers' market along the way.

Follow on social media:
Instagram: @ElizabethHarrisNutrition
Facebook: @ElizabethHarrisNutrition

Sign up for Elizabeth's free 5-day "Discover Intuitive Eating" Challenge:
https://elizabethharrisnutrition.com/5day-challenge

Join Elizabeth's Facebook Community:
https://www.facebook.com/groups/healthandhealingwithintuitiveeating/

Visit on the web:
https://elizabethharrisnutrition.com/

Book a complimentary whole health strategy session with Elizabeth:
https://elizabethharrisnutrition.com/booking

References:

1. Fildes, Alison, Judith Charlton, Caroline Rudisill, Peter Littlejohns, A. Toby Prevost, and Martin C. Gulliford. "Probability of an obese person attaining normal body weight: cohort study using electronic health records." American Journal of public health 105, no. 9 (2015): e54-e59.
2. Mann, Traci, A. Janet Tomiyama, Erika Westling, Ann-Marie Lew, Barbra Samuels, and Jason Chatman. "Medicare's search for effective obesity treatments: diets are not the answer." American Psychologist 62, no. 3 (2007): 220.
3. Cho, In-Jeong, Hyuk-Jae Chang, Ji Min Sung, Young Mi Yun, Hyeon Chang Kim, and Namsik Chung. "Associations of changes in body mass index with all-cause and cardiovascular mortality in healthy middle-aged adults." PLoS One 12, no. 12 (2017): e0189180.

4. Bacon, Linda, and Lucy Aphramor. "Weight science: evaluating the evidence for a paradigm shift." Nutrition journal10, no. 1 (2011): 1-13.
5. Tylka, Tracy L., Rachel A. Annunziato, Deb Burgard, Sigrún Daníelsdóttir, Ellen Shuman, Chad Davis, and Rachel M. Calogero. "The weight-inclusive versus weight-normative approach to health: Evaluating the evidence for prioritizing well-being over weight loss." Journal of obesity 2014 (2014).
6. Wang, Zhiqiang, Meina Liu, Tania Pan, and Shilu Tong. "Lower mortality associated with overweight in the US National Health Interview Survey: is overweight protective?." Medicine 95, no. 2 (2016).
7. Chastain, Ragen. "The Harm of Weight Stigma." WeightandHealthcare.substack.com. https://weightandhealthcare.substack.com/p/the-harm-of-weight-stigma. Retrieved on July 30, 2023.
8. Gaesser, Glenn A., and Siddhartha S. Angadi. "Obesity treatment: Weight loss versus increasing fitness and physical activity for reducing health risks." Iscience 24, no. 10 (2021).
9. McManus, Katherine D. "Benefits of a healthy diet—with or without weight loss." Harvard Health Publishing. https://www.health.harvard.edu/blog/benefits-of-a-healthy-diet-with-or-without-weight-loss-2018121915572. Retrieved on July 30, 2023
10. Wood, Laura. "Global Weight Loss Products and Services Market Report 2021: The Business of Weight Loss in the 20th and 21st Centuries." Cision PR Newswire. https://www.prnewswire.com/news-releases/global-weight-loss-products-and-services-market-report-2021-the-business-of-weight-loss-in-the-20th-and-21st-centuries-301354957.html#:~:text=The%20global%20market%20for%20weight,forecast%20period%20of%202021%2D2026. Retrieved on July 30, 2023.

Chapter 14

THE SWEET SPOT OF IKIGAI

Combine Your Strengths, Experience, and Passion and Start a Business You Love

Emily Reagan

MY STORY

We were doing laps around the Arc de Triomphe. I got angrier and angrier in the backseat of our rented Peugeot, jealous of a female robotic voice inside our Garmin. She replaced my job as the passenger seat navigator and map reader. She didn't know where we were going.

It's not in that direction!

Horns blasting around us.

Let us in, so we can exit!

I knew we were going the wrong way.

We left Paris on our way to Normandy by way of the French Open and headed off in the wrong direction. We just wanted to drive by the famous tennis stadium. She took us east. My husband and father-in-law sat in the front seats and blindly obeyed her poor directions.

We circled the 12-lane roundabout about six times. I was losing my mind.

I've been in this circling pattern before.

At 22, I had no idea what I wanted to do with my life or which direction to go. Who does?

My first plan was to join the Air Force like my fiancé—even received a coveted full scholarship in journalism, only to be rejected during my physical when they found asthma residing in my soccer and volleyball player lungs. Deep down, it was for the best, but it still stung. I shook it off and pursued my broadcast/electronic media degree with a business minor anyway.

Then with four weeks left until my finals, my fiancé got orders to South Korea for an unaccompanied, one-year remote military assignment. *No biggie*, I thought, *I'll wait for him.* But reality sunk in. Without a job or a defined path for my future, what would I do about adult things like medical, bills, and insurance? *Where I will live?* At that time, it seemed easier to get married. Then I'd be on his military orders, and we'd move to his follow-on assignment, Germany, together.

So I did something I said I'd never do.

I got married in college with one month left until graduation.

My husband moved to Korea ten days later. I graduated as a newlywed and alone.

Now what?

Shiny new degree in hand but no real-world experience to make me instantly hirable. Like most coming out of college, I lacked technical skills. A broadcast/electronic media major was fun—an outlet for my creative side where I produced news packages and live videos, wrote TV shows, and created websites with flash animations in my classes. One summer, interning on a TV morning show, stuck doing mostly admin work and witnessing the reality of the news industry, cured me of pursuing that dream.

Self-doubt crept in. *Did I just settle for an M.R.S. degree because I chose to marry in college and follow my husband without my own career in place?*

Determined to be useful, I jumped on opportunities. Every time we moved with the military, I found "for the time being" jobs, many even related to my journalism field. Unfortunately, I started over so many times that low pay and minimal vacation days were my norm. We always moved again before I could work my way up and prove myself.

But it all had an upside.

It forced me to keep looking for my thing. I got scrappy. I sought out ways to build more skills from my talents and college classes. The invaluable experience and confidence gained from doing many seemingly unrelated jobs, bartending, working for HGTV, and substitute teaching, made me adaptable, taught me to make huge pivots on short notice, and learn new things quickly.

Each different task gave me more confidence to put my name in the hat for jobs I'd never done before. It set the stage for bigger things to come and gave me the faith in myself to try anything put in front of me.

In time, I embraced the fact that my career path wouldn't be straight like my college roommates who were climbing corporate ladders, buying homes, and establishing a defined career. I let go of the stigma of having what the world called "the perfect job."

And got a few bruises along the way.

A new boss at a non-profit once told me after he hired me for a role where I'd wear many hats that he was thrilled by all my experience. My heart swelled, and then he said, "I knew I could get you for cheap."

Ouch.

He really meant he loved my valuable experience from all of my previous jobs, but that would be forever overshadowed by my always-moving-away military spouse status. We both knew I couldn't waltz in, completely unknown, to the well-paying energy company down the street and command a six-figure salary. Other organizations passed me by allowing this non-profit to scoop me up for budget-friendly pay.

It stung. But it also empowered me. Rag-tag resumes prove we're well-rounded, capable, and willing. They also show we're not lazy.

Even though we're told our worth isn't tied to what we do, we still desire this intersection of job satisfaction, feeling valued, and being paid well. There's a perfect Venn diagram to explain this formula called the *Ikigai*. Ikigai is a Japanese concept that means "your reason for being," *iki* meaning "life," and *kai* meaning "worth." There are four components:

1. What you love—what you innately enjoy doing.
2. What you are good at—your raw talents.
3. What you can get paid for—the economics of supply and demand in the job market.
4. What the world needs—where you make the world a better place.

It's one thing to pursue a passion but not get paid for it. It's another thing to have a job that pays well but leaves you feeling empty. Then there's the perfect intersection (the *Ikigai*) for each of us that embraces our individual character traits and God-given strengths.

I call this the sweet spot. (It's easier to pronounce too! Ha!)

It's our balance of wealth, satisfaction, purpose, and ultimate happiness. Mine is different from yours, and yours is different from the next woman's. But how do you find your *Ikigai*?

Sometimes you won't until you *experience life.*

I've always been a little envious of those people who knew their college major from the beginning and had clear career goals and visions. I've had friends who knew they'd be doctors. My brothers are pilots. My sister is an engineer. It was clear and obvious to them. But some of us need to get out and experience the world. We need to try new things and gain clarity in the journey, and then bring it all together in a powerful multi-potentialite way.

And that's okay!

We shouldn't beat ourselves up if we end up in a job that's not quite right. Here's your permission to dabble! Your path doesn't have to be perfect or linear, and it doesn't have to make sense. We're allowed to be multi-passionate and multi-talented and explore those themes. It will all come together if you stay self-aware.

Connect with and trust your inner nudges.

I've always been hyper-aware of when I wasn't operating in the zone. My gut tells me when something is off. I don't berate myself when I get those feelings; I simply recognize I've veered off my personal path and adjust. Each and every past work experience took me a step closer to my *Ikigai.* It also taught me that my dream job had to be flexible so I could be there for my family at a moment's notice.

Freedom and flexibility become even more important when we have children.

Once my son was born and we PCSed, I never went back to the office. Freelance work took over. A print shop business owner referred to me needed my help writing press releases (*okay, easy enough*) and doing his social media marketing (*new to me, but hey, I'm really good at figuring things out, why not?*). I wasn't looking for work but said yes to the challenge. That's how I started a freelance digital marketing service business—by accident.

That first client, coupled with all my years doing random marketing, PR, and journalism jobs, gave me the confidence to continue down this path, not knowing where it would take me.

We don't always see our exact path right away. Jumping in with current knowledge and skills and starting small works well. Let your passion reveal itself as your story unfolds.

Little by little, my business grew with me taking on freelance projects and retainer work, helping clients with their social media marketing, media kits, Pinterest, website updates, and launching their digital products. Because of the vast experience in my work history, I had the confidence to say yes to new opportunities. Sometimes I took on projects I'd never done before and had to learn on the way. Clients trusted me and knew they could count on me to get stuff done.

It's scary putting yourself out there, saying yes to something unknown, but the euphoria of figuring it out is candy for the soul.

Before long, my business exploded. My client roster was filled, and my husband was getting ready to deploy for an entire year—and I now had four kids. None of my family lived close by to help out, so I needed to scale down my workload, or I'd burn out.

Then, something clicked.

Many of my fellow overeducated, underemployed military spouses and mom friends were unable to find work, let alone their dream jobs. They lacked confidence and didn't have any connections. Most had taken baby breaks. They were bored, broke, and missing that spark in their life. They were not in their *Ikigai*.

I felt blessed and fortunate that I "made" my own dream job and knew I could help more business owners and women at the same time by being a connector. If I could help these women find their *Ikigai* and introduce them to dream clients, it could be a win-win. The women could find high-paying work in fields they felt passionate about. And biz owners could find their perfect teammate—their unicorn hire! I wanted to be the kind of woman who includes others and brings them up with me.

So I trained a couple of friends. I taught them everything I know about digital marketing and doing freelance client work. I proved the model—that someone could learn everything from scratch, apply it, and turn into a sought-after teammate. I brought them on my team as part of my agency and passed on client work. At one point, I had eight women working with me—one was the commander's wife! She was a friend of mine with an engineering degree who wanted to get back into work now that her daughters were in school.

It felt so amazing to help this woman. She told me how much having a piece of herself back changed her life. It bolstered her confidence and gave her tangible results other than a clean house and worrying about her kids' homework. She knew nothing about digital marketing but was able to use her project management talents combined with my online business and marketing knowledge to be an all-star launch manager and online business manager for one of my clients.

Seeing those women grow, plus the fact that my agency was soon maxed out with work, pushed me to take my next big step. I put myself out there and turned my internal team trainings into a course.

Now more women can see how empowering this work can be. It gives you deep insight into online business—a stable yet dynamic marketplace that is the new future. It gives you tangible experience working on teams and working through projects, deadlines, and tools. It gives you valuable tech experience. It gets women who've been sitting on the sidelines—while having babies or moving or pausing or needing changes—the relevant, in-demand skills to be able to find work.

And the biggest benefit is the confidence factor. When you go out and learn something new, apply it, do it, and get results, it feels so damn good. You tap into your own power and abilities. And you know you can do it again because you did it once. This confidence stems directly from competency. No one can take that away. You carry yourself differently. You attract more clients, opportunities, and new doors open.

You know you can waltz into that energy company down the street and command a position with a matching salary. This is a game-changer.

The marketing piece may not be everyone's *Ikigai*, but it may get you a step closer. You have to try things. You have to put yourself out there and see.

It's like work dating. You have to sample different clients, different work, and different niches to find out what you really love.

For me, this work offers variety. I can use my journalism skills with writing and love seeing my efforts in print as blogs, emails, websites, social posts, marketing funnels, etc. My biggest joy? Helping clients and students find and showcase their strengths.

It works out differently for every student I've worked with. They each have unique combinations of talent, interest, experience, and education. I had one business owner come to me searching for a digital marketing assistant from my course, but she didn't want just anyone. It would help her business if her new teammate also had a teaching background and knowledge/love of art history for her course. How many people do you know love art history? I reached into my student pool and found four women who fit the bill. She hired two.

That's when I realized what these women really were: unicorns. They each had a rare skill set based on their education, past work experiences, interest, hobbies, and passions. I supplied the digital marketing knowledge to help them move into what was in demand (what the world wants to pay for in the *Ikigai*), and they turned into an indispensable teammate.

This dream teammate is hard to find—a mystical unicorn.

It's funny that I picked that symbol; I'm not a girlie girl, but the sparkly unicorn is my mascot because each one of us is unique, and our career stepping stones take us to unique places.

However, you can't compare unicorns to unicorns. It's not apples to apples.

Everyone's distinctive background, education, hobbies, and passions got them where they are today. Like my example of the art history teacher teammate, small business owners often have a hard time finding ideal candidates for their team. They need someone who has the right background, tech skills, and an understanding of online marketing—and also can take care of a couple of key things in their business at the same time: customer service, project management, and marketing. It varies with every business and team setup. There is a business owner out there who needs your skills!

Business owners also want teammates who are adaptable. The most valuable skill you can possess is the ability to adapt to quickly changing environments. It is comfort with ambiguity. And what else does a military spouse's resume show? Ability to evolve. So even if you're starting new, you can trust yourself to figure it out.

Remember that most important soft skill. Use it in your interviews and discovery calls. Tell stories that show you learning new things, figuring it out, and making magic happen. Tap into this strength.

Since founding my business, I've helped 350 women—and a few awesome men—learn digital marketing implementation skills through my Unicorn Digital Marketing Assistant School. I teach them the foundations of digital marketing and the technical skills to help clients with content marketing, email marketing, affiliate marketing, and marketing funnels. Then I help them start their freelance business and get their first paying clients.

It's everything I wish I would have had when I was starting out.

Now I'm a six-figure business owner, putting my past salaries to shame. I have the flexibility in my schedule to put my family first and to do the work that lights me up. I'm in my *Ikigai*. I'm being paid to use my brain, be creative, write, design—and tell my clients what to do. Finally, I'm a true, behind-the-scenes maven. I help clients with digital marketing, assisting them as they build their sales funnels, monetize their talents, and launch their products.

I want to encourage you, dear reader, to take it one step at a time. You may not have it all figured out when you're 22, 42, or any other age—and that's okay. The key is your awareness and ability to take action when something doesn't feel right. Don't be complacent. Don't settle.

And that's why I'm here with these Leading Ladies. I want to help women find their sweet spot on the *Ikigai* so they can live life with their purpose and get paid well for it. I want to help women open new doors to the future of freedom, flexibility, and wealth.

I want you to find your *Ikigai.*

THE PRACTICE

Finding your Ikigai

Below, I've outlined how to start finding your *Ikigai.* Grab a notebook and pen, and journal about each of the following questions. Take some uninterrupted time to reflect and dive into them. Don't censor while you write; let your answers just flow.

FIND WHAT YOU LOVE:

What did you want to be when you grew up?

What do your friends say you're good at?

What's something you did as a kid that you were naturally drawn to and loved?

What are things in your past jobs you hated doing?

What do you enjoy doing in your spare time?

What's something you'd do for free and not care if you got paid?

FIND WHAT YOU CAN BE PAID FOR:

List ten online skills and abilities you already have.

List five specific skills related to previous industry/education.

List five work/character strengths that would benefit a small business owner.

You've got a great start by answering these questions, and you probably see patterns emerging, like a love of drawing and graphic design skills. Find jobs that pay for those talents, and you'll find your Ikigai.

Learn about Emily's digital marketing courses and programs, or submit your job opening for a marketing assistant at https://emilyreaganpr.com/

Emily Reagan is a mom of four, digital marketing implementer, and founder of the Unicorn Digital Marketing Assistant School.

As a scrappy military wife who's moved every two years, Emily has worked in various jobs related to public relations, marketing, sports media relations, journalism, and video production. Finally, her random skill set paid off as a freelance digital marketer. She helps creative entrepreneurs take their talents online, grow and nurture their audiences and build their sales funnels. She's worked behind the scenes of 102+ businesses.

With her rare PR and marketing background, she quickly booked out and didn't like turning down clients, so she trained her smart over-educated, underemployed military spouse and mom friends to learn digital marketing tech skills and take on clients as their own.

She calls her UDMA School graduates "unicorn" because they have all the rare resourceful qualities, online insight, and marketing implementation skills that online business owners are desperate to have on their teams... aka that total magical package.

Emily's all about giving women options. She encourages women to have their own independent source of income and start their own freelance businesses to capitalize on the part-time, remote work opportunities and change their future.

As a practitioner, she also works with clients in VIP days to build marketing funnels, create content marketing plans, set up affiliate programs, write podcast pitches, and more using her unicorn skill set.

Emily currently lives in Richmond, Virginia, with her four children and new sheepadoodle Pepper. She loves Nancy Drew, good coffee, and coaching her kids' sports teams as sporty spice

Connect with Emily at:

Website: https://emilyreaganpr.com/

Instagram: @emilyreaganpr.

Chapter 15

BE A WOMAN WHO HAS (NOT DOES) IT ALL

Learning How to Use Your Resources and Network

AliceAnne Loftus, Business and Leadership Coach

MY STORY

Being a woman who "has it all" without feeling the pressure to "do it all" is about achieving balance, fulfillment, and satisfaction in all aspects of your life. It involves recognizing that you can prioritize and excel in different areas without sacrificing your well-being and happiness. Sounds impossible. Right?

I'll tell you a little secret: you must learn to utilize your network. Now before you close the book and shout, "I hate networking!" I want to point out that "networking" isn't a dirty word. I admit I spent years avoiding networking; I always felt salesy and cheap as I attempted to plug my business and get people to understand what I do in a thirty-second infomercial. It doesn't feel authentic to me to strike up a conversation and feel that I have to convince someone of my value, credentials, worth, or purpose in hopes that business will be shared or exchanged.

As the Leading Lady community continued to grow, I recognized its potential to become a formidable network for women leaders. When you learn to effectively leverage your network, it can be a transformative experience, both personally and professionally. A robust network can open doors to countless opportunities, offer much-needed support during challenging times, and provide valuable insights and knowledge. I realized that I had previously been networking incorrectly. I was networking in ways that I thought everyone networked, but I was learning that networking is about relationships and developing strong bonds with like-minded professionals who share common values.

Given that many of the members were business owners or organizational leaders, I saw an opportunity to harness this collective strength. Encouraging them to share their businesses, services, and products led to a magical transformation—the flourishing of economic support and business exchanges within the community, all while women were also finding resources, services, and products that supported them in profound ways in their lives.

The atmosphere buzzed with enthusiasm as the members eagerly engaged in doing business with each other. An exciting trend emerged: the community was not just fostering connections but also becoming a powerhouse of economic empowerment. The women were thrilled to support fellow women-owned businesses, and the community provided a platform where such companies were recognized and elevated to the forefront. In a world where women often have to fight relentlessly for acknowledgment and recognition, this became a haven where they confidently showcased their ventures, were celebrated, and knew that their contributions mattered. The community's spirit of collaboration and mutual support fostered an environment where women felt they belonged, regardless of their background or location. It transcended geographical boundaries and served as a testament to the collective strength of women in business and leadership. This unity and encouragement made the Leading Lady community an empowering space for women to thrive and realize their full potential. Furthermore, it challenged the narrative that a woman must do everything in her business independently. Suddenly, all these women were sharing their challenges *and* solutions with one another, highlighting that while none of us are experts at everything, there were many experts in the community on just about anything.

Initially, women didn't join the group with the primary intention of making sales. Instead, they sought to establish personal connections centered around shared experiences as women leaders. They engaged in discussions about business and leadership, finding comfort and common ground, and even forming friendships. However, as the saying goes, "People do business with people they know and trust," I witnessed this truth unfold. Through their interactions, the women in the group built friendships, formed professional relationships, and learned to trust one another. They realized they weren't alone in their challenges, and often there was another woman who could help them by providing advice, a service, or a product to help them find a solution. When one woman faced challenges with accounting in her business, she sought help and guidance by posting a question. An accountant spoke up and stepped in to offer valuable advice. These exchanges sometimes transitioned to private conversations where a genuine connection occurred, and in some cases, the accountant was hired to provide further assistance. Yes, it's vulnerable to admit to needing help; however, in the admittance and acceptance that you can't do it all, an opportunity to outsource, connect with another woman, and even support another business unfolds.

Moreover, the ripple effect of these interactions was evident. Others who saw the advice shared in the group might contact the original poster to inquire if they had received the help they needed. There's a shared empowerment in the vulnerability that we all face similar challenges. When one woman speaks up about struggling with something, others experiencing similar struggles pay attention. They relate to and appreciate the open discussion. They shared perspectives, possible solutions, and positive experiences, leading to more opportunities. This cycle of support and collaboration demonstrated how the group evolved into a space where members could rely on one another personally and professionally. The group became a fertile ground for establishing trust and credibility. The women fostered a community where their businesses and skills were recognized and valued by offering genuine support and assistance. Women were no longer isolated in their own pursuits but connected in the reality that we could all succeed with support and encouragement. The connections were not solely transactional; they were built on mutual understanding, respect, and shared experiences.

As a firm believer in the power of relationships, I saw how these authentic connections contributed to the success and growth of the women in the group. The women were embracing the idea that it's not just about the products or services they offered; it's about the authentic connections they forged with others. This mindset led to meaningful partnerships, increased business opportunities, and a stronger sense of belonging within the group. We showed we could implement balance, feel greater fulfillment, and find deeper satisfaction in our leadership roles by leaning on each other for support, sharing knowledge and experiences, engaging in problem-solving, and even outsourcing. The entire process unfolded naturally and organically, driven by a constant desire to help and support one another rather than being solely focused on making sales. The group's primary emphasis on building trust and nurturing relationships created an environment where personal and professional growth seamlessly integrated, making it an empowering and unparalleled space for women in business and leadership.

As for the big lie that we stand alone against the world, the jig was up. We all knew that together we were better. We aren't meant to do this alone; we need each other. Through our combined strengths, talents, and skills, we could be more productive, fulfilled, and happier in our lives. With continued support and collaboration, we can lead fulfilling lives and achieve success while acknowledging we don't have to handle everything alone.

Remember the woman that was seeking accounting help? She shared that she specialized in creating websites during her conversation with the accountant. The accountant immediately recognized an opportunity to amplify her business and help open a door.

"I have a friend in need of a website for her new business! I have to connect her with you!" Recognizing the expertise and trustworthiness, the accountant decided to connect them.

This networking and mutual support led to more fruitful connections and collaborations among the members. Through these ongoing connections and relationships, the women grew their businesses and enhanced their credibility within the community and beyond. They built a reputation as reliable and accomplished professionals in their respective fields by continuously supporting one another. The process exemplifies the power of authentic networking and demonstrates how it contributes to each member's overall growth and success.

As the network expanded, so did the opportunities for collaboration and referrals, creating a positive cycle that further strengthened the community. Ultimately, the women elevated their businesses and built a collective reputation for excellence and reliability. The group's focus on trust, credibility, and connections sets it apart from typical business networks, making it a unique and empowering space for women in business and leadership to thrive. The evolution of this group went from connection to friendships, community to network, and credibility to sales.

As you can imagine, groups showing sales evidence attract more people whose only interest is sales. Now, hear me out: There's nothing wrong with wanting to grow your business. There's no shame in trying to market yourself and land a deal. Sales are a genuine and essential aspect of our companies. The bottom line, without sales, there's no business. However, let's not forget that making sales and closing business deals are not the foundation of why I built the Leading Lady community. I wanted women to have an opportunity to share their businesses, but I didn't want genuine relationships to be overshadowed by sales pitches.

Preserving the community's integrity and ensuring its focus on relationships, leadership topics, and shared resources was paramount to me. To maintain a balanced environment, I introduced special promotion days on the first day of each month. Additionally, I created specific posts and threads for women to share their businesses, services, and products while keeping the group's essence centered around leadership, inspiration, and encouragement. When non-member businesses were referred to, I'd offer the reminder, "Our primary goal is to support our fellow Leading Ladies and empower each other." I go on to share this analogy:

Imagine you sell apples and services related to apples, and you go to a party where you're confident that people are able to share their products and services. You have, in fact, joined this party with the promise and expectation that you could network with the other partygoers. You're standing with a group of women, and everyone is sharing what they sell and what types of services they offer.

"I sell oranges as well as equipment to make high-quality orange juice," one woman shares.

"That's fantastic! My company sells pineapples, and we even have a line of mixers that complement the flavor; we should collaborate!" another woman says enthusiastically.

"I sell apples and all things related to apples!" you optimistically contribute.

Moments later, another woman joins the group and says, "I've been chatting with partygoers all evening, and I can't find anyone that can help me secure apples for an event next week."

Here's your moment! Here's the perfect opportunity for you to share your business, and these women know what you do, too, so they'll help plug you. Now before you can even speak up, one of the women standing there says, "Oh, I'll connect you with my neighbor, Johnny! He sells apples and all things apple-related." The music comes to a screeching halt (like one of those record players making that ear-piercing scratching sound), and you look dumbfounded and amazed that you're standing right there, and an opportunity passes over you.

"Our primary goal is to support our fellow Leading Ladies and empower each other," I repeat. "We're here together to support one another. Look for the resources and opportunities within the group, and if you cannot refer another Leading Lady, then take the conversation outside of the group or offline."

Upholding these boundaries wasn't always easy, but I knew it was crucial to maintain the group's integrity and ensure our members had a welcoming space to engage.

The Leading Lady community has blossomed into a robust network for women leaders, transcending the traditional boundaries of business relationships. By focusing on building trust and fostering authentic and meaningful connections, the community became an empowering space where women thrive both personally and professionally as leaders in their own lives. The women know they can have a life where they have it all because they see a network that can help them through unwavering support, encouragement, and resources to fill in where needed. The women have shown that true empowerment comes from lifting each other up, celebrating each other's successes, and creating a culture of mutual trust and respect.

As we continue to grow and welcome new members, I'm committed to preserving the essence of the Leading Lady network—the emphasis on community, connection, leadership, and shared resources. By upholding these values, we will ensure that the group remains a haven where women can confidently showcase their ventures, be celebrated, know that their contributions genuinely matter, and know that they are never alone in their endeavors. Together, we have built something remarkable—a network that empowers women in business and leadership and exemplifies the true power of collaboration, trust, and authentic relationships.

As we move forward, let us continue to support each other, uplift one another, and create lasting impacts on each other's lives and businesses. I'm excited to see what the future holds for the Leading Lady community and the incredible women who make it what it is. Thank you for being a part of this journey, and here's to the boundless potential and opportunities that lie ahead as *we lead* the way for transformative growth and success through networking and collaboration. Remember that "having it all" is not about doing everything perfectly but aligning your actions with your values and finding contentment in the journey.

By cultivating balance, prioritizing self-care, utilizing your network, and seeking resources, you can become a woman who confidently and authentically embraces her version of "having it all" without being a woman that feels she's stuck "doing it all."

THE PRACTICE

Whether you're just starting to build your network or looking to maximize your existing connections, here are some strategies on how to best utilize your network to achieve your goals:

Identify Your Goals: Before leveraging your network, define your objectives. What do you want to achieve? Whether seeking a new job, expanding your business, or gaining industry insights, clarifying your goals will help you focus your networking efforts. Set achievable and realistic goals for different areas of your life, such as career, family, relationships, health, and personal growth.

Goal 1:
Goal 2:
Goal 3:
Goal 4:
Goal 5:

Build Authentic Relationships: Networking is not just about collecting contacts; it's about building authentic relationships. Take the time to get to know people beyond their professional roles.

List three to five women you would be interested in getting to know better:

1.
2.
3.
4.
5.

Schedule a coffee or lunch date. Don't talk business; show genuine interest in their lives, aspirations, and challenges. Building rapport and trust lays the foundation for a meaningful network.

Prioritize self-care: Make time for self-care and well-being. This includes getting enough rest, engaging in activities that bring you joy, and taking care of your physical and mental health. Remember that taking care of yourself is essential for giving your best to others.

What are three things you will do for yourself?

1.
2.
3.

Be a Giver: Be generous with your time, knowledge, and resources. Offer help and support to others without expecting anything in return. People are more inclined to reciprocate when you need assistance when you give freely.

Giving the gift of connection (a referral) is sometimes the best thing you can do for someone's business.

Share three to five referrals of companies you have worked with in the past year.

1.
2.
3.
4.
5.

Be Visible and Active: Stay engaged with your network regularly. Attend industry events, workshops, and conferences to meet new people and strengthen connections. Actively participate in online communities and social media platforms related to your field.

- Is there a conference that you would like to attend in the next six months?
- What online communities do you participate in? How often do you post or engage in discussion?
- What networking groups would you like to become more involved in within the next twelve months?

Nurture Existing Connections: Regularly check in with your contacts to see how they're doing. A simple email, message, or phone call can go a long way in maintaining relationships. Celebrate their successes and offer support during challenging times.

Check-in with five contacts:

1.
2.
3.

    4.
    5.

Leverage Social Media: Social media platforms like LinkedIn, Instagram, and Facebook offer excellent opportunities to connect with professionals in your industry. Share valuable content, join relevant groups, and engage in discussions to establish yourself as a thought leader.

- Update your profile, picture, and bio.
- Do an audit of who you are following and who follows you.
- Engage with whom you want to form a deeper connection.

Set boundaries: Establish clear boundaries to manage your time and energy effectively. Learn to protect your personal time and avoid overextending yourself.

What boundaries would you like to implement and hold yourself accountable to? Make a list of three to five:

    1.
    2.
    3.
    4.
    5.

Seek Advice and Mentorship: Don't hesitate to ask for advice or mentorship from experienced professionals in your network. Most people are willing to help and share their knowledge with those who show genuine interest and respect.

Who are three people you admire in your industry? What guidance would be helpful from each person?

1.
2.
3.

Schedule a phone call or meeting to ask them about their story and if they'd be willing to share any advice or guidance with you.

Join Professional Associations: Professional associations are a valuable resource for networking and skill development. Consider joining relevant organizations in your industry to expand your network and access exclusive opportunities. Associations whose mission speaks to you or you feel passionate about are another way to deepen your network meaningfully.

Make a list of associations or organizations you'd like to learn more about and possibly join. Make a point to visit at least three associations in the next six months.

List:

Offer to Collaborate: Collaboration can lead to new opportunities and visibility. Look for ways to collaborate with individuals in your network on projects, events, or initiatives.

List three to five potential partners you could collaborate with in business:

1.
2.

3.
4.
5.

Reach out and schedule a coffee or lunch date to discuss collaboration possibilities.

Delegate and ask for help: Don't hesitate to delegate tasks or ask for support when needed. Sharing responsibilities with others can ease the burden and allow you to focus on your priorities, whether at work or home.

What areas of your life (personally or professionally) need to be outsourced or delegated?

1.
2.
3.

Who can you ask for help with each of those items?

1.
2.
3.

Stay Informed: Keep yourself updated on industry trends, news, and developments. Knowledge allows you to contribute meaningfully to discussions and positions you as an informed and valuable network member.

What are three current trends in your industry? Why are these important to know?

1.
2.
3.

Ask for Introductions: If there's a specific person or company you want to connect with, don't be afraid to ask for an introduction from someone in your network who knows them. Personal introductions carry more weight than cold outreach.

- Who do you want to meet?
- Who is in your network that could introduce you?
- Schedule a call and ask for an introduction.

Offer Testimonials and Recommendations: If you've had a positive experience with a colleague or business partner, offer to provide a testimonial or recommendation. Positive feedback can enhance their credibility and strengthen your relationship.

Leave five to ten testimonials and recommendations for businesses you have worked with. Be sure to ask them where they would like you to leave reviews. List their names here for accountability:

1.
2.
3.
4.
5.
6.
7.
8.
9.
10.

Be Open to New Connections: Embrace diversity in your network. Connect with people from different industries, backgrounds, and experiences. A diverse network can offer unique perspectives and enrich your own knowledge.

Make it a point to meet five new people and learn about their businesses. Try to find people from industries you're unfamiliar with or have no experience with.

1.
2.
3.
4.
5.

Learn to say "no": Recognize that you don't have to take on every opportunity or responsibility that comes your way. Saying "no" to commitments that don't align with your goals or values allows you to focus on what truly matters to you.

What are three things you need to say "no" to or stop participating in?

1.
2.
3.

Foster a support network: Surround yourself with supportive and understanding people who lift you up and encourage you to pursue your goals without judgment.

List five people you know you can count on and have shown up for you in the last six months.

1.

2.

3.

4.

5.

6.

Write them a thank you note and tell them how much you appreciate them!

By implementing these strategies, you'll transform your networking efforts into a rewarding and fulfilling experience, propelling you toward achieving your goals and establishing lasting connections that enrich your personal and professional life. With determination and the right approach, you can unlock the full potential of your network and make significant strides towards overall achievement, balance, and happiness.

WE LEAD TOGETHER
How to Guide Your Path to Success

AliceAnne Loftus

Repeat after me, "I am not meant to do this alone."

Say it loud and proud with sincere conviction. "I am not meant to do this alone."

Breathe it in, hold it in your heart, and exhale.

That's exactly how I feel in a room with the Leading Lady Ambassadors. The number of times I've sat at a table with these incredible women and looked around as we held space for each other, radiating love, gratitude, and solidarity. The comfort and peace of being surrounded by these types of women is invaluable. There isn't judgment, insecurity, or pretenses. We show up ready to share, celebrate and grow together. Sometimes we show up raw, unfiltered, messy, broken, confused, stuck, and lost. Regardless, we show up ready to receive and ready to give. Give what we can and receive what we need. Never in my life have I felt so connected, so supported, and so valued. I knew that this was something special. I knew that it had to be shared with others. It had to be shared with all.

What excites me the most about this book is the fact that here we are, women I've worked with for years, sharing our stories, skills, experiences, knowledge, and insight not only to teach but encourage, inspire, and uplift each other in ways that can and *will* immediately impact each reader in profound ways. This is a book that you can come back to a thousand times. I hope the pages are dog-eared, highlighted, underlined, and have scribbles of notes in the margins. This book is meant to be a reference guide, a tool kit, and a direct line to and for women who know that when we work together, powerful things can happen.

As you use this book, know that each author is extending an open invitation to be a resource to you. Please reach out and contact them directly. Explore the various ways they can support you in your own journey. Whether it's personal growth or professional advancement, each ambassador is dedicated to excellence and has proven time and time again that she is committed to the success of others. Let this be a guide to highlight the various resources available, the power of a robust network, and the importance of collaboration and community. Join the ambassadors' online communities, reach out to ask questions, and trust that if they do not immediately know the answer, they will connect you with someone who will.

As you lead your way through your life, remember that you are not alone. We are a community. *We lead* each other. *We lead* together. *We lead* to strengthen each other. *We lead* to inspire and be inspired.

ACKNOWLEDGEMENTS

Special thanks to my husband, Marty, for reminding me that I'm not someone that gives up on myself, a project, or my community. You always believe in me and constantly remind me to believe in myself.

Thank you to my business coach, fellow author, friend, and Leading Lady Ambassador, Erin Harrigan. Your coaching, encouragement to lean into my prayer, and accountability to not let myself play small have been the anchor that has kept me grounded in my mission.

To Jennifer Osterhouse, my friend, fellow author, and Leading Lady Ambassador, for the beautiful cover design and her relentless commitment to push herself to grow, learn and take on new skills and endeavors. Thank you for challenging yourself, being curious, and being brave.

Sincere gratitude to Laura Di Franco for breathing new life into this project and making every step along the way seamless. Your knowledge, expertise, and guidance will forever be appreciated.

Finally, to every single Leading Lady Ambassador and author in this book, I am beyond grateful. You truly put the *best* in "Business Besties." Our friendship is invaluable to me. Your dedication to this project, its mission, and the empowerment of women in business and beyond is inspiring. Thank you for your unwavering support, continued trust, and commitment to outstanding excellence.

Join The Leading Lady Community

www.leadinglady-coaching.com

https://www.facebook.com/groups/LeadingLadiesAAL

*"Every woman's success
should be an inspiration to another.
We're strongest when we cheer each other on."*

SERENA WILLIAMS

Made in United States
North Haven, CT
15 November 2023

44048578R00143